POTPOURRI, INCENSE
and other
FRAGRANT CONCOCTIONS

POTPOURRI, INCENSE

and other

FRAGRANT

CONCOCTIONS

Ann Tucker Fettner

WP
WORKMAN PUBLISHING COMPANY
New York

LIBRARY OF CONGRESS CATALOGING IN PUBLICATION DATA
Fettner, Ann Tucker.
Potpourri, incense, and other fragrant
concoctions.

1. Perfumes. 2. Incense. I. Title.
TP983.F38 1977   668'.542   77-5931
ISBN 0-911104-97-6

Jacket photo by Jerry Darvin

Potpourris shown on cover courtesy of Aphrodisia.

Jacket design by Paul Hanson

Book design by Barbara Bedick

Workman Publishing Co.
1 West 39 Street
New York, New York 10018

Manufactured in the United States of America
First printing May 1977

10 9 8 7

We gratefully acknowledge the kind permission to reprint from the following:
"Words For The Wind" from *Collected Poems* by Theodore Roethke.
Copyright © 1955 by Theodore Roethke. Reprinted by permission
of Doubleday & Company, Inc.
"The Rose Family" from *The Poetry of Robert Frost* edited by Edward Connery
Lathem. Copyright 1928, © 1969 by Holt, Rinehart and Winston.
Copyright © 1956 by Robert Frost. Reprinted by permission
of Holt, Rinehart and Winston, Publishers.
From *Paterson*, Book V by William Carlos Williams. Copyright © 1958
by William Carlos Williams. Reprinted by permission
of New Directions Publishing Corporation.

For Peter
and David

My thanks to
Harvey for his idea   Alice for her work
Steve for his care   They made it bloom.

CONTENTS

PART I: THE ART

THE NATURE OF SCENT   13
  Description of Terms   15

THE ELEMENTS OF PERFUME   20
  Main Scent   21
  Blenders   22
  Fixatives   22

PERFUME INGREDIENTS   24
  Flowers   25
  Herbs   35
  Spices   43
  Woods   45
  Grasses, Roots, Mosses, and Resins   46
  Animal Essences   50

EXTRACTING THE SCENTS OF FLOWERS 56
    Extracting Essential Oils 58
    Making Tinctures 59
    Scents by Distillation 60

PART II: THE RECIPES

POTPOURRI 65
    Dry Potpourri 66
    Moist Potpourri 82

SACHET 91

BATH POTPOURRI 98

TOILET WATERS 100

INCENSE 103
    Solid Incense — Basic Recipe 108

SCENTED CANDLES 114

ROSE RECIPES 118

POMANDERS 121

PART III: INTO THE KITCHEN

125

Citrus and Mints   128
Oils   130
Herbs   130
Teas   132
Addendum: Herb Smoking Mixture   132

PART IV: SCENTED PRODUCTS FOR FUND RAISING

133

SOURCES

139

PART I.

THE

ART

THE OLD POT-POURRI JAR

THE sun is down and the daylight past
    And the fire is burning low,
And through the gloom of the ancient room
    Dim phantoms come and go.

They are conjured up by the subtle scent
    Belonging to days afar,
Which my fingers press, from the deep recess
    Of an old pot-pourri jar.

There, hand in hand, down the long oak room
    A youth and a maiden pace—
And I know love lies in the youth's dark eyes,
    While they rest on the maiden's face.

Across the spinnet's long silent keys
    I can see fair fingers sweep,
While from it arise low harmonies,
    And I bow my head, and weep;

Till steps and voices destroy the spell,
    And I dry my foolish tears,
And the youth and maid and the old airs fade
    Back into the bygone years.

They were conjured up by the subtle scent
    Belonging to days afar,
Which my fingers press from the deep recess
    Of an old pot-pourri jar!

HELEN MARION BURNSIDE.

THE NATURE
OF SCENT

A late rose ravages the casual eye,
A blaze of being on a central stem.
It lies upon us to undo the lie
Of living merely in the realm of time.

THEODORE ROETHKE

I have an herb patch called Mad Heriot's Garden after an aunt who lived in the early 1800s. In the voluminous family correspondence of the time, she was referred to only once; "Of Heriot, outside of her 'beloved flower garden,' I will not speak." As southerners have traditionally tolerated eccentricity with aplomb, I have always assumed Heriot to have been extraordinarily peculiar. If so, how grand that she had "her beloved garden;" she still has.

We learn as we grow that time is far more than a series of "nows;" it encompasses the enormous bolt of all-time, and into the present space we try to pull those memories which we have found pleasant. There is no better way to recreate the past than through our sense of smell.

The stimulation of our sense of smell and its effects on the mind and emotions and behavior is little understood. It is thought that incoming odors are screened by the nervous system centers and automatically graded in such a way as to steer us towards or away from the stimulus. Noxious and putrid odors repel us; absence of odor produces no stimulation; pleasant ones attract us. When what we smell is spicy and dry, we are excited to action; the narcotic scents of flowers and drugs relax us into reverie. The odors of food, except when we are ill or full, attract and please us, perhaps the only area where the sense of self-preservation through smell is still at work for man.

Other animals have a much more highly developed sense of smell. They are lured by the odor of a flower, or of a potential mate, and will travel great distances in search of the life-sustaining, life-continuing object. Certain female moths emit a mating odor to which we are entirely insensible, yet which, within a short time, will draw all male moths of that species from more than a mile away. Animals and plants use their scents for purposes of procreation. We take advantage of this biological reality and use these scents for our own pleasure.

DESCRIPTION OF TERMS

The effect of a fragrance on one person may be entirely different on another: Ten people inhaling the same aroma would probably perceive and be affected by it in as many different ways, so much does a smell depend on the mental association it evokes. If I describe lily-of-the-valley as having a beautifully sweet, delicate fragrance, there is no way to be sure that you will find this true for yourself.

In early spring, I have walked through a shaded field of these flowers when the dew was still sparkling. Well rested and wearing a particularly pleasing dress, I found their fragrance delightful. Had I had an argument with someone I loved under those same trees with the scent of lily in the air, their aroma would probably strike me as overly sweet and cloying. My grandmother could not stand the scent of gardenia bushes in bloom because when she was a child the way to the outhouse was lined with the shrubs. Their odor brought back memories of loss of sleep, cold mornings and rain. She would not visit me when my bushes were in bloom, so unpleasant did she find the fragrance of their waxy white blooms.

How can mere language make sense of this amorphous range of effects and impressions? How can one "describe" a perfume? People have tried for thousands of years. Fragrances have been equated with the musical scale, with the highest note on the treble clef assigned to civet. The lowest tone was said to correspond to patchouli. Each chord formed a bouquet. The bouquet of C chord in the bass was formed of sandalwood, geranium, acacia, orange flowers and camphor; G chord in the treble was sweet pea, violet, tuberose and orange flowers again. An old book, *The Garden of Herbs*, tells of a peasant from Breton who came to

Paris to give a concert of perfumes; he was laughed at as a lunatic.

Although the musical equation doesn't work unless we all know music—and are in complete agreement on odors as well—there is a close analogy between the art of perfumery and music. The careful development and building of one note or fragrance on another should result in harmony.

The creation of perfumes has also been compared to landscape painting. The main scent is the primary feature or intent of the painting, the blenders are the combination of colors and the fixatives represent the background. Details such as birds in the sky, the refraction of light from a stream or rock and the small foreground details add life and spice to the finished creation. In other words, we are simply trying to develop an atmosphere, an aid to the imagination that will transport our minds into a slightly different time and space.

The overpowering perfumed incenses used in old religious and magical rites were designed to do just that—to help the participant into a spiritual world and put him in touch with whatever gods or devils he sought.

The best definition of categories comes from the German master-perfumer, Dr. Paul Jellinek, who devoted his life to creating a psychological basis for the formulation of perfumes. In brief, here is how he grouped and described the scents we work with:

1. **Sex-stimulating:** Animal and other similar odors—such as costus root and amberette seed—have this quality in perfumes. They are blunt and alkaline and may have a fatty or waxy overtone. Often, they are slightly rancid-smelling alone. In perfumes they impart a "low" base note, a "dark" quality.

2. Narcotic or Intoxicating: The fragrance of flowers and balsams are best described this way for they have a sweet, mellow scent. This quality in high concentrations, such as pure otto of rose or another essential oil undilute, tends to cause headaches and, sometimes, slight nausea. Properly mixed in perfume products, they have the ability to dull our senses slightly and cause a general sense of relaxation. The next time you are in a flower shop, take a moment to feel this happening to you.

The scent of drugs from natural substances such as opium and hashish also has this sweet, mellow, perhaps "soft" fragrance. Most of the flowers we use have this effect, but only the blossom in most cases. The rest of the plant falls into another category.

3. Anti-sexual or Refreshing: These fragrances are in direct contrast to the animal odors. They are the "green" resin fragrances produced by the saps and leaves of plants, by camphors, pines and some of the mints. Eau-de-cologne with its base of citrus oils is a good example. These fragrances, when used as the signature of a product, give it a "healthy," clean feeling. Most after-shave lotions are formulated with this in mind; the signature is a "wake-up" note rather than a relaxing one.

4. Spicy and Bitter: Most vegetable materials with the exception of flower blossoms fall into this area. Seeds and roots and stalks and some leaves have a bitter, dry effect. Mosses and woods fall half-way into this category; a few like santal share some flower overtones. These odors have the ability to wake and move to action; they are businesslike, activating.

A number of substances fall between and share these categories: A honeylike smell is both sweet and fatty; a few flowers have a spicy, invigorating effect like lavender; some fruity odors are acid and sweet at the same time. But generally speaking, these four groups should guide you in deciding what elements you want and what general proportions to use. Categories 1 and 3 are in direct contrast to one another as are 2 and 4. You would cancel out the effect if opposing categories were evenly balanced. Having once decided what effect you want to achieve, judicious additions from the other categories will make for a more interesting and effective perfume.

Your product's future use is a good guide to making your decision. You might want a bath potpourri with a soft, mellow fragrance. A basket of rose petals for a bedroom might demand a stronger animal note than one for the living room. To perfume a closet that holds outdoor clothes you would want a different quality than for a drawer in which you keep lingerie. The base quality of an incense can be piney and fresh, or sultry and heavy depending on your taste.

Jean Jacques Rousseau said that the sense of smell is the sense of imagination. A violet alone isn't exciting. If you can find a way to set it by a stream, and make that stream bubble, you've created a small world for yourself and others to enjoy.

THE ELEMENTS
OF PERFUME

"It is not the object of perfumery, and very rarely the object of individual perfumers to follow the slogan *L'art pour l'art* by imitating nature. It hardly needs pointing out that women, who are the major consumers of perfumery products, have no ambition to smell like natural violets or roses."*

How true! When perfumery learned to synthesize scents and was able to manufacture exact floral duplicates, the sale of such scents as "rose" and "violet" dropped dramatically. While we find these fragrances in association with their flowers almost irresistible, segregated from the blossom they lose some of their appeal . . . some actually smell quite unpleasant.

The appeal of a successful perfume—whether it comes from one of the great French houses or from your own

*From *The Practice of Modern Perfumery* by Paul Jellinek, published in 1954 by Interscience Press, New York.

workroom—is the result of an artful combination of ingredients. One scent alone does not make a perfume, and is no more exciting than the smell of fresh orange on your fingertips. Moreover, a single fragrance will have no staying power.

Some of the perfumes sold today are made with as many as a hundred ingredients; others incorporate only a few. Whatever their secret, however, all include the three basic elements—main scent, blenders and fixatives—essential to the bouquet of an original, long-lasting perfume.

MAIN SCENT

The initial decision when making a perfume is what the main, or signature, scent is to be. Personal preference, of course, is your first criteria, but keep in mind the type of product you are concocting, its intended use and the availability of ingredients.

Many fine perfumes have as their signature an evenly mixed group of scents whose end products may be described as "New Mown Hay" or "Sachet Reine" (the favorite of Queen Isabella of Spain). Some approximate the scents of growing things; others are creations unlike anything in nature. For your early efforts, I would suggest selecting a scent with which you are familiar, one that you like to have around you. This main scent is the key: All else that you add is to modify and enhance it, to make it more delicate or rich and to fuse the fragrances into a single, coherent theme.

BLENDERS

Blenders are the additional scents that are combined with a main fragrance. Their role is secondary, but important, for they give harmony and maintain balance in a mixture. Almost anything can be used.

In a potpourri or sachet, blenders can be minute quantities of woods, little seeds, bits of herbs, spices, flowers and leaves; or they may be tiny pieces of citrus rind and drops of essential oils. All of these will mingle with and enhance the original idea. When you make a perfumed product, such as toilet waters, bath potpourri, or incense, your blenders will be the essential oils from flowers and plant parts as well as finely pulverized mosses and, in some cases, woods and roots.

FIXATIVES

The third element to add is a fixative, an animal or vegetable substance which blends into the other scents, adds its own note to the main fragrance, and, most importantly, has the ability to fix and hold the overall perfume for a long time. Fixatives have been well used in the past. Perfume jars from ancient Egyptian tombs, unearthed and opened after several thousand years, still emit fragrance. Although we do not know how the Egyptians succeeded in fixing their scents to last so long, we do know that a well-mixed, well-fixed home product should retain its perfume for years.

Scents are volatile—they evaporate readily. Without a fixative, they will waft up and away from the flowers and oils; the fixative releases the scents slowly and economically. Certain fixatives work particularly well with specific scents. Orris root, for example, has an affinity for lavender. Other good combinations will be noted later in the text.

PERFUME
INGREDIENTS

The perfumed concoctions described in this book—potpourris and sachets, incense and pomander balls, bath potpourris and toilet waters—can be made of flowers, herbs, seeds, fruits, spices, woods, mosses, roots, resins—of any or all of these, or of the essential oils that are extracted from them. These materials in themselves are a great source of satisfaction: a pleasure to grow or search out, a delight to handle and to smell. Familiarity will also help you determine what fragrances hold particular meaning for you.

In creating perfumes, it is possible to use any of hundreds of ingredients: They can be broken down into categories, but one may end up with as many classifications as there are scents. To simplify matters, I prefer to divide the materials into animal and vegetable, and the vegetable into a number of separate groupings. Flowers, of course, top the vegetable list.

FLOWERS

Kama, the Indian god of love, is depicted, like Cupid, with bow and arrows. The bow is of sugar cane with a string made of bees, and his five arrows are each tipped with the blossom of a flower which pierces the heart through the five senses: One of the five flowers is **jasmine.** Introduced into the world of flowers by the Arabs, somewhere in time lost, jasmine has long been a perfume favorite. Ladies in the East roll its blooms in their hair at night so their tresses and skin will be fragrant throughout the next day. When combined with lotus and asoka plant, it is thought to be an aphrodisiac by the Hindus. "Schnouda," the whitening cream mentioned in *The Arabian Nights*, is made of jasmine pomade and benzoin. The Orient uses jasmine extensively as scent and as a fragrant addition to tea with which it blends deliciously. The most fragrant flowers come from the *Jasminum odoratissimum.* All jasmine grows in warm climates; all have a delightful, heavy scent.

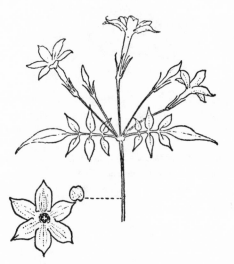

When first introduced to this exotic flower, Charles Dickens actually went into rhapsodies: "Is jasmine then the mythical morn, the center, the delphi, opthalmos of the floral world? Is it the point of departure, the one unapproachable, indivisible unit of fragrance? Is jasmine the Isis of flowers with veiled face and covered feet to be loved of all, yet discovered by none? Beautiful jasmine, if it be so, the rose ought to be dethroned and the inimitable enthroned in her stead. Suppose we create a civil war among the gardens and crown the jasmine Empress and Queen of all!"*

Dickens aside, the **rose** need fear no loss of status, for of all the flowers used by perfumers, the rose is queen. "The rose—Oh, no man knows through what wild centuries roves back the rose. . . ."** This lovely flower, most written of in history, folk medicine and poetry, forms the basis for many perfumed products.

The rose is said to have been given to the god of silence by Cupid to seal a promise not to reveal the love of Adonis and Venus. Its origin was the blood of Adonis; it is under

*From *Book of the Scented Garden* by Frederick Burbidge, published in 1905 by John Lane: The Bodley Head, London and New York.
**From the poem *All That's Past* by Walter de la Mare.

the celestial sign of Venus. A symbol for secrecy and silence as well as for love, it was once used as the sculpted motif on the ceilings of banquet halls to remind diners that what was said *sub vino*—under the influence of wine—was also said *sub rosa*—under the rose and not to be repeated. In later times a fresh rose was often hung over the dining table to remind guests that the conversation was to remain in confidence.

In ancient times, rose petals were scattered under the feet of heroes; whole flowers were worn around the necks of celebrants, and rose water was sprinkled on guests entering the house. The first written records of the flower are found in the *Iliad* and *Odyssey*, and Horace and Pliny give suggestions for its cultivation. The word "rose" comes from the Greek *roden*, meaning red, and it is thought that once the flower's only hue was a deep, dark red. But over the centuries it has been cultivated for color, form, fragrance, number of petals, recurrent bloom, size of blossom, length of stem, resistance to disease and fragrance of leaf. It has mutated into what some experts estimate to be as many as 250 true varieties. Roses that are as small as a little button or as large as a cabbage can be grown in a range of color from almost black through all shadings of red and pink to palest lavender to yellow to clear white.

The flower is a member of the order Rosaceae to which many of our most useful, attractive plants belong: the genus *Pyrus* includes peach and pear, apricot, almond, apple and others in the fruit family. Smaller members of this group include blackberry, strawberry, raspberry, bramble and hawthorn. These plants are scattered across the world, growing profusely in almost all temperate zones. The rose is highly adaptable to climate within its range, is easily crossed and, with a little care, simple to grow.

The rose is a rose,
And always was a rose.
But the theory now goes
That the apple's a rose,
And the pear is, and so's
The plum, I suppose.
The dear only knows
What will next prove a rose.
You, of course, are a rose—
But were always a rose.

ROBERT FROST

For the nominal gardener who buys bushes at the garden or grocery store, here is a general description of the types of roses that are best for perfumery. When selecting a bush, look beneath the popular name of the rose for the genus (usually in small, italicized print). One of the best scent roses is the cabbage rose, *Rosa centifolia*. The Provence rose also falls in this group. Look also for *R. gallica* which includes the apothecary rose and rose de Provins. The genus *canina* includes the dog rose and wild briar. All roses descended from the *damascena* are highly scented. Roses with any of these pedigrees produce fine fragrance but many other varieties do also. Even some of the varieties with fruitlike scents as well as the unscented types can be used for appearance and bulk in products like sachet and potpourri.

Some of the very popular roses do not have the distinctive aroma that we have come to think of as rose-scent. Rather, they approximate their fruit cousins—apples, melons and apricots. A few have a lilac odor and some smell like hyacinths. The popular Peace rose has a musky, heavy fragrance as do several others. But if you get involved with growing roses for their perfume, stick close to the *damascena* family for it is from this group that the powerful "otto" or attar of rose is taken. The Kazanlik rose, grown in the East, is the best supplier of otto—10,000 pounds of petals are required to make one pound.

Rose bushes need lots of sun and protection from strong winds. They shouldn't be grown under eaves and trees where accumulations of rain water will drain on them. The soil for their cultivation should be firm, well fertilized and well drained. During the growing season they must be sprayed once a week with liquid fertilizer mixed with an insecticide that keeps off the rusts and mites that can ruin the blossoms. They also need plenty of water around their bases. After the growing season is over, they must be prepared for winter according to the temperatures to which they'll be exposed.

A book about roses is a worthwhile investment if you are serious about the quality and longevity of your plants. A more rewarding flowering plant hasn't been found. With thoughtful selection and care, roses will bloom from early spring right through fall in most areas. As their flowers come to bloom, they can be gathered, treated and stored for delightful perfumes for the cold season ahead.

Orange blossoms are among the most fragrant of all flowers. Driving through the center of Florida during the blooming season is truly heavenly, for the air is perfumed with an almost painful fragrance—one which holds not only the image of the delicate, waxy flowers that are giving up their perfume, but suggests the promise of endless fruits and sweet leaves. Except for the flowers, the trees that bear the finest fruits have inferior essential oils. The perfumer must go to the bitter orange for the oil called neroli, (also referred to as bigarrade). This oil forms the base of all eau-de-cologne and is produced from the rind of fruit. Another oil, petitgrain, is extracted from the leaves of the bitter orange tree.

If you live in a climate where orange and other citrus grow, you will probably have a little trouble finding bitter oranges, as the trees are useful only for shade or for grafting with other citrus—their fruits, lumpy and sour, are usually allowed to ripen and fall. But if you cannot get fresh bitter orange, the essential oils of this and other citrus can be purchased. You can also use the peels of the oranges, lemons, grapefruits, tangerines and limes that you bring home from the grocer. Don't neglect these rinds, chopped and dried as flavorful additions to cake icings and candies; and tangerine peel, dried, is a fragrant part of many good Chinese dishes.

Tuberose, a wild flower from the East Indies, is one of the sweeter perfumed flowers. It grows from a bulb planted in the fall that flowers the following spring. It is said to produce exactly two full-blown flowers a day which, if they are to be used for their fragrant oil, must be gathered immediately on opening. The plant grows about three feet high and the flowers are fragile-looking, white, elongated "tubes" which open into a six-petal star. They are attractive to grow in a garden and make a graceful scented addition.

Acacia is a flowering shrub, a small, decorative tree that grows in hot climates. It takes about five years to produce flowers, but when it does, you'll be pleased you waited. The foliage is a feathery, emerald green and the flowers are tiny, fuzzy, golden buttons. The flowers produce a slightly violet odor, but are sweeter and quite strong. Because of this scent, acacia has also been one of the best perfume flowers since early recorded history. In 565 A.D. it was listed with benzoin as the fragrance to be offered to Jove. A lovely poem about Indian girls shows their fondness for this colorful, aromatic tree: "Fond maids, the chosen of their hearts to please, entwine their ears with sweet sirisha [acacia] flowers whose fragrant lips attract the kiss of bees that softly murmur through the summer hours."*

You can sometimes buy acacia buds dry from herb shops but they are quite expensive. If you live in a warm locale, you might investigate growing several of these trees. They are small and one of the loveliest specimens around. The botanical name is *Acacia farnesiana.*

"To know whether a man who has been severely beaten will recover or not, take the violet, bruise and bind about the forefinger: if he sleeps he will live, if not, he will die. You should ascertain this before you interfere with the case."**

Violets, aside from the legends about them, have a dainty, universally liked, light odor. Although it is faint, the fragrance is distinctive and pleasant and the various waters and perfumes of the violet—whether from the flower or its close odor-equal, orris root—are always popular, though not as much today as in Victorian times.

*From *The Book of Perfumes* by Eugene Rimmel, published in 1865 by Chapman and Hall, London.

**From *The Magic of Herbs* by C. F. Leyel, published in 1926 by Jonathan Cape Ltd., London.

These charming low woods plants grow wherever there is enough water and shade. Their scent disappears when dried, but they can be pressed and their shape and remaining color make a nice addition to whole-flower potpourri.

Two popular bulbous flowers are **jonquil** and **narcissus**. They are so easily grown or bought that I have included them, but mostly for bulk in dried, whole-flower products, for their odor is very transitory and not a favorite of everyone. You can buy oil of narcissus if you like its earthy, sweet note.

Mignonette is an extremely fragrant annual that is mostly grown in Africa. Its oil has a heady, sweet odor and mixes beautifully with the orangelike aroma of bergamot.

One of the sweetest garden flowers is the **gardenia.** The creamy satin-finish blossom lasts only a day or so but if you live in a temperate zone, you can have several bushes to perfume the spring air. Oil of gardenia isn't one of my favorites; it's almost too sweet, but many people love it. The flower is useless when dried as it turns a sad-looking tan. Unfortunately, most white flowers suffer this same fate as soon as they dry. **Baby's breath,** which is easily grown from seed, is one of the exceptions.

If you live in a southern climate you can grow and use flowers such as **lotus, magnolia** and **oleander** for scent and appearance. Oleander is good only for bulk as its scent, never strong, fades rapidly. You must also be careful with the plant around children as all of its parts are poisonous. Magnolia flowers also turn dark but the petals of this dish-sized blossom can add an interesting touch to potpourri. This is the crowning tree of the South, prehistoric relic that grows to great heights of both size and beauty. Lotus and oleander are really wet-southern plants and grow best in places like Florida. The lotus is the mystical flower of India and has figured in many legends and as an important design element in paintings and sculpture from the East. It was used as one of the toxic additions to poisons as far back as 1200 B.C. Lotus has a decidedly animal component to its fragrance; if you like it, you can buy the oil.

Both the **lilac** and **honeysuckle** have distinct and very popular aromas. They can be grown in cold climates for garden perfume, but are not of much use in perfume except in essential oil form as they develop strange qualities as they fade. Lilac has a high indole component (discussed later) which makes it, when fading, rather decayed smelling.

Lily-of-the-valley is one of my favorites. The scent is so sweet and penetrating in a bouquet on the dining room table that you can't taste the food. But it's worth giving up meat and potatoes once in a while to sniff your way to fullness. This exquisite, half-wild plant has dark green sword-shaped leaves and delicate little white bells growing up and drooping from a long, central stalk. If grown in the shade with plenty of water, it will grow and proliferate almost like a weed. For larger flowers, the roots should be dug up and divided every three years. This little plant has been used as an element in perfume, medicine and cosmetics for hundreds and hundreds of years, and in perfume, contributes a delicate, ladylike fragrance.

Wallflowers were to England what Confederate jasmine was to the South in the days when families lived in the same home for generations. The sweet vine produces a flower with an airy scent which can be added to your perfumes as oil.

There are hundreds of other flowers that may be added to dried, whole-flower mixtures such as potpourri. Anything you find pleasant, whether found in the woods, grown in the garden, or bought from the florist, can be used for bulk and color in dry mixtures. The best combinations are often found through experimenting with whatever is available. However, only the rose, lavender, citrus flowers and tuberose hold their scents after drying, so most will be used in dry form for show, appearance and bulk. If you become interested in extracting essential oils from flowers, almost anything with a scent that pleases can be tried. Fragrant blossoms that yield a perfume to use in flower waters and colognes and such are discussed later. Now we go on to the next group of growing things and their scents.

HERBS

Lavender, one of the world's favorite flowers, can well be listed here as it has the aromatic quality associated with the herbs. Classically, lavender belongs to England. Of all the places in the world, this island is where it grows best and is most loved. A delightful old book, *The Magic of Herbs,* has this to say of it: "Our grandmothers distilled it, and made it into sachets to scent their linen cupboards, and our great-grandmothers quilted it into their caps and cured every disease under the sun with it. Its clean and fragrant perfume was acceptable alike to Puritan and pagan. William Turner extolled it as a cure for colds and as a comfort for the brain, and advocated its use in indoor headgear, it was the gayest color the Quakers were allowed to wear, and it scented the ruffles of the Court exquisites."

We get the word "lavender" from the Roman *lavare*, to wash. They used it in their baths, presumably to sweeten their bodies, as there was no such thing as soap at the time. Like the rose, lavender has long been a most popular flower to grow and to use. Its perfume from both growing and dried plants is sweet, aromatic and strong. It has been an essential ingredient of medicines down through the centuries.

There are three kinds of lavender, any of which can be grown in your garden. If you can't grow it, it is easily and inexpensively bought in dry form. It adds both fragrance and bulk to dry perfumes. The most fragrant, delicate lavender is true or English lavender (*Lavandula vera*) which is also quite hearty. Spike lavender (*L. spica*), though not quite as strong as English lavender, yields three times as much oil. These two are equally good for the garden. The third type is French lavender which is a smaller plant and not for cold climates.

When growing these plants, you have a choice of either good or bad soil: The bad yields smaller plants and less attractive flowers but far finer oils. In good soil, the plants and flowers blossom beautifully but at the expense of the fragrance. Lavender grows best from cuttings and, ideally, the roots should be dug up and divided every few springs. If unattended, the plants will still grow for years.

No plant is more deserving of garden space. They remain a manageable size—from one to three feet depending on climate—have a fragrance second to none, and are lovely to look at. The great bonus is that you can pick the tiny flowers from the spikes and use their perfume in all sorts of ways. Even a small paper bagful sitting on my desk makes the area fragrant with a clean, fresh, friendly scent that seems to soothe troubles away.

In this aromatic group fall all the lovely, useful mints: **peppermint, spearmint, orange or bergamot mint, wintergreen** and **white mint.** Bergamot and white are the two

most used in perfumes; the others make many appearances in mouthwashes and other products which need their antiseptic, cleansing odors and tastes. The oils of bergamot and white are available in herb stores and fancy pharmacies. Many perfume recipes will call for the bergamot as its fruity scent adds greatly to that of flowers.

All mints are easy to grow and make ideal house-herbs. They thrive in large window boxes and will take over the ground when planted outside. They grow low on creeping roots and most, when they flower, have purple-toned blossoms. Their scent both growing and dried is lovely, refreshing and piquant. In dried perfumes you have to be careful to keep the mint scent below cooking levels; otherwise, you will make a perfume more redolent of good things to eat than one attractive to the opposite sex.

The leaves of the **rose geranium,** one of our common house plants, carry in them one of the strongest, most useful scents available. The plant is easily found at the nursery, costs little, and is simple to grow if kept well drained and given plenty of sun. It grows beautifully indoors or out and has been used for years and years to give a roselike fragrance to many cosmetic preparations. One of the old scent books described the difference between its flowers and leaves by saying the fragrance of the leaves is "ready if sought," meaning that flowers will literally come after you with their sweet odors; leaves you have to go after yourself. Grow some rose geraniums even if you don't plan to use them to make anything; a few leaves, the bigger the sweeter, can be crumpled to perfume a room. All members of the geranium family have scented leaves and all mix well with verbena and lavender.

Patchouli is included here because of its aromatic fragrance. Small and neat, this little Indian plant produces a powerful, strange-smelling oil which was used to scent shawls and linens during the early days of British trade with that country. You can obtain oil of patchouli and occasionally dried flowers if you like the odor. It is not pleasing to everyone as it has a rather off-beat, heavy bouquet. The essential oil smells rather like a musty attic.

The herbs we *think* of as herbs comprise a formidable group. They are used routinely for cooking purposes, but all are used for perfumes as well. Many of these small fellows can be grown in your apartment if you're moderately careful about giving them the right amount of room, sun and proper drainage. All are garden plants.

Most herbs grow naturally and well in very poor soil; a basic cause of failure in their culture is oversolicitude.

Don't fertilize and coddle herbs; let them dry out between waterings. Like dogwood trees, to grow which from small trees it is said, you have to speak harshly and occasionally give them a kick, herbs will flourish without fussing.

Rosemary is quite lovely. Very old plants grow to considerable size, but young plants are small. The tiny blue flowers, on close inspection, resemble miniature orchids. But if you want to grow rosemary, take this old message into consideration: "Lavender and rosemary is as woman to man and white rose to red. It is an Holy tree, and with folk that been just and rightfulle it groweth and thryveth."*

*From *The Magic of Herbs* by C. F. Leyel.

Hippocrates wrote of this plant and the Romans took it into England. It has been used all through history as an important ingredient in beauty and health preparations. The Queen of Hungary is supposed to have used a distilled essense of rosemary in her bath every day and so beautiful was she at seventy-two that the enchanted King of Poland begged for her hand. This perfume water, Hungary Water, is the oldest known and is still being made. It is said that if you wash with water in which rosemary has been boiled and let the air dry your body, all signs of age will pass away.

Rosemary might also be added to smoking mixtures as a substitute for tobacco. A recipe is given on page 132.

The name of this pleasant plant seems to have come from its love for growing near the sea—the best still grows in England—*ros* meaning dew and *marinus,* of the sea. Perhaps the name is an allusion to its pale, silvery-blue flowers as well as its love of moisture.

Thyme and **marjoram** are two more important herbs in perfumery. Two of the thymes are commonly used in perfumery: *Thymus azoricus* and *T. zygis.* They are both neat little plants that are beautiful and useful in a rock garden or border. You need a very large window box for them as they like to creep around over rocks. These plants need good drainage and lots of sun and grow best in a sandy soil mixture. *Azoricus* has a lemony odor and lilac-colored flowers in the summer. *Zygis* is paler with gray-green leaves and lavender flowers.

Sweet marjoram is a hardy little plant with narrow green leaves and white flowers which have a piney scent. It needs a great deal of sun and is relatively slow growing which makes it a grand border or inside plant. One of the early real whiskeys used marjoram for flavor and was called "Golden Water." Marjoram was also one of the important additions to early pomanders (more on those later) and a popular Greek perfume used it with quince blossoms. It is said that no one who had sold his soul to the devil could abide its smell.

Basil is just the opposite. Folklore calls it an evil plant, dedicated to Satan. Some rather strange properties have been attributed to this easily grown plant. A certain Italian in the Middle Ages was said to have "bred a scorpion in his brain" by smelling basil too much. And "To make sure that women shall eate of nothing that is set upon the table, take a little green basil and when men bring the dishes to the table put it underneath them, that the women perceive it not: for men say that she will eate of none of that which is in the dishes whereunder the basil lieth."

I must have a scorpion in my brain because I am never without basil plants. In summer, they grow outside to the size of bushes. The stems get woody and the plants produce a profusion of spikes with tiny white flowers around which bees always swarm. So many leaves do two basil plants produce that you get in the habit of picking a few just for sniffing. It will grow in the worst conditions in the house, though not so tall, and the plants will last for months if the flowering spikes are kept plucked off. Save these for potpourris; dry the leaves for seasoning all Italian foods and use them fresh in anything that calls for tomatoes.

Seeds of **coriander** have a number of fragrant uses, particularly in flavoring liqueurs. They are also one of the principal ingredients in lily-of-the-valley perfumes. Coriander was first mentioned thousands of years ago, and in tandem with parsley, henbane and hemlock was burned to produce a whole army of demons. Perhaps the reason for its evil influence is the way the growing plant smells. When young, both the seeds and plant, which has a graceful, pink-white, lacy flower, have a perfectly awful odor. The seeds become fragrant when they mature but because of its early characteristic, coriander isn't a plant for a closed space. By all means invest in coriander seeds from an herb store. As the signature in a sachet they are delightful and longlasting, fruity and sweet-smelling; and they are relatively inexpensive.

Lemon verbena is an old-fashioned garden plant with delightful, fragrant lemony leaves. It can be garden- or house-grown, though it does best outdoors. Its graceful foliage is a pleasant addition. Called vervain in olden times, verbena was said to keep one from dreaming if one drank its juice or hung a sprig around the neck. Mixed with lavender and sweet geranium leaves, verbena was used in little bags hung on arm chairs in the Victorian era to sweeten the visitors' impressions of a room. Folklore tells us that the Druid women wore it in crowns on their hair.

Dill, fennel and **caraway** are three other herbs you can grow. Their seeds produce oils that are sometimes used in perfumes. Caraway and dill have lovely, lacelike umbrella flowers and the fennel's foliage is feathery. All are important plants for the kitchen and have been used for hundreds of years in medicines. Pythagoras wrote that a stem of dill held in the hand would prevent epilepsy. And of fennel, a thirteenth century medical book admonished, "He who sees fennel and gathers it is not a man but a devil."

All of the preceding herbs can be garden-grown and many are for your window box and roof garden as well. The last three are available at the grocery; crush a few seeds and see what they suggest. The following cannot be grown but can be purchased either whole and dried or in essential oils.

Cubebs are small spicy berries from an East Indian shrub which is a member of the pepper family. They have been used for hundreds of years in some bizarre love potions and recipes as well as for perfumes. They figure in this fascinating account of love potions in *The Arabian Nights:* "After hearing Sham-al-Din's story he [the druggist] betook himself to a hashish seller of whom he bought two ounces of concentrated Roumi opium and equal parts of Chinese cubebs, cinnamon, cloves, cardamoms, ginger, white pepper, and mountain Sheik [a lizard which is supposed to serve as an aphrodisiac]: and pounding them all together boiled them in sweet olive oil: after which he added three ounces of male frankincense in fragments and a capful of coriander seed, and macerating the whole made it into an electuary with Roumi bee honey. Then he put the confection in a bowl and carried it to the merchant saying, 'Take of my electuary with a spoon after supping and wash it down with a sherbert made of rose conserve: but first sup off mutton and house pigeon plentifully seasoned and hotly spiced!' "

SPICES

A whole raft of spices we use in the kitchen are also important ingredients in perfume products. When adding them or their oils to your concoctions be frugal; it is easy to end up with a basketful of rose petals that smells like a fruitcake. Clove, cinnamon and nutmeg are the major spices for perfumery and each has a long history.

Cloves are the unopened flowerbuds of an evergreen tree that grows in India and Africa. The very best come from the island of Zanzibar. A friend traveling there tells me that balls of clove are routinely hung in homes for their perfume. In the Molucca Islands, no one is allowed to wear a hat near a clove tree that is in flower for fear the tree will become alarmed and refuse to bear fruit.

Oil of clove has been included in all mixtures used to treat illness; the scent is so powerful, so healthy, that it is able to drown almost any other odor. Use cloves or oil of clove to spice up and enhance "lively" mixtures and always with carnation with which it is extremely compatible.

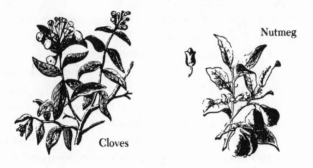

Nutmeg

Cloves

Mace and nutmeg also come from an evergreen tree native to the Moluccas. The nutmeg is the seed which is used whole or ground. Mace comes from the seed's covering. They both have a spicy scent and were used in the eighteenth century with opium and wild crabs and saffron as a medicine.

Cinnamon and cassia, its less-used cousin, are made from the bark of trees that are members of the laurel family. Cinnamon perks up many flower odors and can be used either powdered, as an essential oil, or in larger pieces, depending on what you are making. It was dedicated to the god Mercury in 565 A.D. and the Greeks described a golden city in the Elysian Fields as having emerald walls, ivory pavement and cinnamon gates.

More fragrance can be had from vanilla, tonquin beans and oil of bitter almond.

Vanilla is the pod of a lovely creeper that grows best in Mexico. The oil has a sweet, mellow odor. Since it is a familiar scent, it is a good one to work with . . . in very small quantities. Don't use the extract you have for cakes and cookies.

Tonquin beans are the fruit of a South American and West Indian tree. They can be ordered in small quantity and add a fruity note to your mixtures. The odor of the bean comes from the presence of coumarin, also a component of **sweet woodruff**. If you like the aroma, the latter can be grown in your garden. A delicious low groundcover that thrives in the shade, it has tiny white starlike flowers and attractive foliage.

Bitter almond scent is made from the crushed nuts after all the oils have been pressed out. It is sometimes useful in oil form and adds a fruitlike scent to perfumes.

WOODS

Anyone who has enjoyed an evening by a campfire or stood near a lightning-struck tree knows the sweet fragrance of wood. An essential source of scents, many trees, especially in the East, are perfume factories in themselves. The most sought after is **santal**, a soft, white wood from eastern Asia. It is hard to find but worth the effort if you are making anything with roses. Its sweet, woody fragrance is a perfect complement.

Easier to buy but less fragrant are the **sandalwoods** which come from Australia, the West Indies and Asia. Sandalwood is a hard red-toned wood which is ground for incense and whole-leaf mixtures. It imparts a sharp, bitter note to perfume.

Both **cedar** and **American sassafras** yield fragrant oils but are less useful, as their woody tones can be overpowering. The cedar, often used to line storage chests, smells pinelike and a bit antiseptic; the sassafras is very spicy.

GRASSES, ROOTS, MOSSES AND RESINS

Several balmy grasses from the East are used in making perfumes. **Lemon grass** has a verbenalike scent and is a pleasant addition in oil form when available. **Ginger grass** is another Indian grass with a geranium scent. Referred to as Kusa-grass, in the Vedas, it was once used as the bed for sacred fires. Its oils have been used to cut otto of rose, but not to good effect. Lemon grass is easily grown in the summer. In Florida I have seen it with swordlike blades over six feet long (1.82m), drooping and fluttering in the breeze. Crushed, it emits a sharp, lemony odor and was, before our journey into chemicals, the prime insect repellent of the semi-tropics. If a recipe calls for them, similarly scented oils can be substituted.

Oakmoss and **reindeer moss** are two lichens that have their own distinct, dry odors and are often used in sachets and bath potpourris. They have the ability to fix and hold the scents with which they are combined. You can sometimes buy them in whole form, in which case they must be washed, dried and ground into powder before using.

Orris root, the most important root used in perfumery, comes from the iris (also called white flag and florentine iris). It was used before Christ by the Romans and Greeks and throughout the East as a fixative and in incense. When dried, it has a delicate violet odor and is an important component of so-called "violet" perfumes.

First grown commercially in Italy, iris is now one of the most popular flowers in gardens around the world. Once planted, the root, or rhizome, will produce flowers for years and years. Plants grow best when dug up and divided every three or four years. The iris needs a lot of water and grows well in the shade. The delicate-looking but good size flower produces incredibly fragile, damp-feeling petals of pale blue. Some petals grow upright and meet each other; others droop down to form a skirt. The leaves are strong, green, sword-shaped and very fibrous.

Of principal concern to the perfumer is the rhizome which is dried and either sliced, powdered or ground to fix the scents of other flowers. It is the most frequently called-for fixative and easily grown by anyone with a shady spot in the yard. If you can't grow it, you can buy orris root in drug or herb stores.

If you dry your own orris root, cut it in small pieces while it's fresh. Once dry, it is as hard as a rock. By the same token, be sure what you order from the herb store is chopped fine or, for sachets, ground; if it comes to you whole, it's impervious to breaking down.

Calamus is the rhizome of another iris, **sweet flag.** This type needs a great deal of moisture and grows happily with one foot in a stream or pond. Calamus can be used with or instead of orris root but its violet odor is not quite so strong.

Vetiver or **kus-kus** is the third rhizome we use. It grows wild in India and was used to scent linens woven there. The famous perfume "Mousseline" was named after the fragrant muslins and is a close match to the plant's fragrance. In India, this root is often shredded and woven into mats which are hung over windows. During very hot weather, water is sprinkled on the mats, thus cooling and perfuming the air.

Of all the substances found in nature, resins, the sticky gums that ooze down tree trunks, are the most aromatic. Their scents quite literally fill the air. When you drive or walk through pine country, particularly when they are tapping for turpentine, you see great drops and lumps of resin glistening on the tree's bark. Even in smaller plants, the resins in the stalks contain the strongest and most lasting odors. Hashish is the resin collected from the flowers of the hemp plant and the jewelstone; amber is petrified resin from prehistoric trees. Often, these beautiful, golden stones will contain a perfect little insect, trapped forever when the resin was still like glue.

Frankincense and **myrrh** are two resins that have always figured in history. Both are written of in the Bible and were significant commodities of ancient trade for religious rites and for personal perfuming. Frankincense, also called olibanum, is from a tree that grows in India and in Arabia or Yemen. Myrrh comes from Arabia and Abyssinia. According to myth, it was produced by the tears of the daugh-

Frankincense (*Boswellia thurifera*).

ter of the King of Cyprus who had been turned into a shrub. The Bible mentions it as one of the two substances used in the embalming of Christ.

In Exodus XXX, Moses said of making holy oil: "Take unto thee sweet spices, statce [thought to be myrrh], and onycha and galbanu; these sweet spices with frankincense of each there shall be a like weight: and thou shalt make it a perfume, a confection after the art of the apothecary tempered together pure and holy."

Herodotus wrote that Arabia was forced to pay a thousand talents of frankincense to Babylon each year, and Ovid recommended it as a cosmetic saying that if it was agreeable to the gods, it could be no less useful to mortals.

Frankincense comes in small transluscent yellow beads, sometimes clumped together. It has a sharp, sweet balsam odor when burned. Myrrh comes in little rough pieces of brownish orange. It is sweeter and less woodsy than frankincense. Neither are used in perfumes today except as incense: The Catholic Church still uses frankincense as the chief ingredient in theirs.

Two other resins, **balsam of Peru** and **balsam of Tolu** come from South and Central American trees and are seldom to be had any more. This is too bad as their fragrances are light and airy and of considerable value in incense. If you can find an essential oil of one it is definitely worth buying in small quantities.

The Biblical benjamin bush now called **gum benzoin,** comes from Thailand and the Indian Islands. Chinese hunters of the coveted birds' nests for soup used to burn this at the entrance to the deep, dangerous caves in which they searched. It is a greyish-brown gum most readily available in powdered form. It adds a powerful aromatic note to dry mixtures and has considerable quality as a fixative for other scents. We use it extensively in many perfume concoctions and it is easily purchased from any supplier of perfume makings.

From a small Asian tree comes **storax** which is used mostly for its fixing properties. Like the other balsams, it has a "dark," "low," perhaps "sad" fragrance that adds a base note to perfumes.

All of these resins have the ability to fix and hold and release the scents with which they are combined and, in many cases, they add their own fragrance to concoctions; none, however, are as powerful and effective as the few we obtain from animals.

ANIMAL ESSENCES

By themselves, undilute, animal essences are perfectly awful. But used with sensitivity, they add a "low" note, an erotic animal quality. If kept below the level of conscious appreciation, most people find their addition quite pleasing.

Musk, the oldest and most widely used of these substances, comes from a pocket under the belly of the male musk deer, an inhabitant of the high mountains in China and surrounding countries. Raw, this substance is so overwhelmingly unpleasant to the nose that, according to one early explorer, the scent of it pure would cause hemorrhage and death. We are never exposed to musk in its pure form, but even in a half-dilute state it is powerful enough to give some credence to this report.

Centuries ago, however, tastes were different. The Chinese used this precious substance—they called it *shey heang*, "deer perfume"—in its strong state throughout their history, despite the fact that their inclination and talents in this area have always been toward incense. As

Musk Deer (*Moschus moschiferus.*)

musk is regarded as a true aphrodisiac, it has been put to some fanciful uses. The Koran speaks of paradise as being full of nymphs of great beauty who are created not from flesh and blood, but from pure musk—as is the earth on which they walk. A nineteenth-century writer commenting on this paradise doubted that it "would prove a great allurement to our Europeans with their nervous tendencies." One is inclined to agree. Several Eastern mosques were built with musk mixed in with the mortar and after hundreds of years the buildings are said to be still redolent of the fragrant stuff.

A cure for melancholy in the sixteenth century was made of musk along with apples, santal, sugar, silk, lapis lazuli, pearls and gold leaf mixed together in rose water . . . somehow. A precious mixture indeed. But musk is precious enough in itself and once introduced into Europe by the early explorers, was used extensively. What we now get is mostly synthetic musk, the cost of the natural being prohibitive.

We include it for the heavy, aromatically sweet and sensual quality it adds as well as for its extraordinary lasting power. It holds its own and other fragrances for an extremely long time.

When you begin making perfumes the temptation is to be able to *smell* every addition. I did this with musk. It simply jumped across the fine line between background and conscious odor and completely took over—and not so pleasantly; the roses were finished, the potpourri basket a disaster. Musk is generally available in tinctures. Be sure to use it in small quantities.

When a vegetable odor is described as "musky," it usually means that it has a powerful, penetrating odor. Actually, only two plants have this real musk scent. One, **costus root,** is seldom available. The other is **amberette** or **musk seed** which can be purchased. There are also several flowers that have the chemical component, indole, which is part of the real musk complex. It is indole that causes wilting lilacs and jasmine to give out a decidedly erotic perfume on a very hot day.

Ambergris, obtained from the sperm whale, is a yellowish substance produced by a disease in the animal. It is found floating near the shore in Japan and other Eastern countries. Sometimes it appears as far north as Greenland and on the western shores of South America. It has been in use throughout history and one wonders at the daring of the first person to pick up and use a lump of this waxy exudate for perfume.

No matter how unattractive the source, ambergris is one of the pleasantest scents used in perfumery. It has a delicate, earthy, balsamlike odor that blends well with almost any scent combination. It does not take over like musk. In the Middle Ages it was thought to be a remedy for the plague. It gave its name to the then-popular pomander balls carried by many dandies (*pomme,* the French for apple, and amber). Later in the text you will find recipes for pomander balls. The great French *cordon bleu,* Savarin, liked it in hot chocolate. Ambergris has always been considered an aphrodisiac in the East where, with musk, it was often drunk in various concoctions.

Civet, another valuable addition to the perfumer's arsenal, comes from an unlikely looking small cat which inhabits Africa and India. From a pouch, the cat secretes a substance which is scraped off and collected: The animals are often kept captive for their perfume contribution. Civet in perfume mixture has a delicate, sweet floral odor and is unexcelled as a fixative. But take care. Use it even more cautiously than musk, as the slightest overuse has a ruinous effect on perfumes. It was widely used during the Middle Ages as a perfume for gloves and other fine leather goods such as book bindings. In London in the 1700s one of the popular shops was called, "At the Sign of the Old Civet Cat."

Civet Cat (*Viverra civetta*)

Castorium, obtained from the perineal glands of beavers, has a natural affinity for leathers. In fact, its odor is reminiscent of a warm arm covered in fine leather. It has a decidedly "masculine" scent and is the basis for perfumes like Russian Leather. It is seldom sold for use by home hobbyists.

Although all of the animal tinctures are comparatively expensive, they are used in such small quantities that you should include at least one in your perfumery plans. They add scent and greatly extend the life of whatever product you make. They can't be used for items such as bath powders and face preparations, but for purely-for-odor enjoyment one of them is essential.

> "the cranky violet
>   like a knight in chess,
>   the cinque-foil,
> yellow-faced-
>   this is a French
>   or Flemish tapestry-
> the sweetsmelling primrose
>   growing close to the ground, that poets
>   have made famous in England,
>   I cannot tell it all:

Slippered flowers
        crimson and white,
                balanced to hang
on slender bracts, cups evenly arranged upon a stem,
        foxglove, the eglantine
                or wild rose,
pink as a lady's ear lobe when it shows
        beneath the hair,
                campanella, blue and purple tufts
small as forget-me-not among the leaves.
        Yellow centers, crimson petals
                and the reverse,
dandelion, love-in-a-mist,
        cornflowers,
                thistle and others
the names and perfumes I do not know.
        The woods are filled with holly
                (I have told you, this
is a fiction, pay attention),
        the yellow flag of the French fields is here
        and a congeries of other flowers
as well: daffodils
        and gentian, the daisy, columbine
                petals
myrtle, dark and light
        and calendulas.

                WILLIAM CARLOS WILLIAMS

EXTRACTING
THE SCENTS
OF FLOWERS

How you use the many plants described in the preceding section depends on what you plan to make. Whole flowers, petals and leaves are particularly desirable for dry potpourri as they lend—in addition to their scent—color, shape and texture. For incense, sachet and bath potpourri, you would use ground or powdered materials. All perfumed concoctions benefit from the addition of an essential oil of one material or another to bolster their scent, as many flowers lose their scent when dry. Actually, many scents from other parts of the world are only available in oil form or in tincture (oil in alcohol). The alcohol makes the tincture more volatile—it gives up its scent more quickly.

You can purchase oils—and other botanicals or forms of botanicals—in herb stores, health food stores, old-fashioned drug stores, and fancy pharmacies. Local drug stores may carry them too, or perhaps can order them. If you are unfamiliar with local sources, check with nearby botanical gardens or look in the classified telephone directory under Health Food Products, Herbs, Flowers—Preserved and Florists, Oils—Essential, Perfumes—Raw Materials and Supplies, Sachets, and Spices. At the end of the book, I include the names and addresses of my three primary sources for these materials.

Though few perfumers take the time and trouble to do so—and few have enough blossoms to make it worthwhile—it is possible to extract your oils yourself. Some are easier than others. You could try your hand at rose or orange or lavender oil, or something from one of the roots. For large quantities of "waters" or cologne, these do quite nicely.

The discovery of oil or otto of rose happened accidentally, as so many marvelous discoveries do. In the 1590s, a canal was dug for the wedding festivities of a Persian princess and the waters of this canal were covered with tons of rose petals. When the bridal pair went rowing on this fragrant water, they discovered an oily scum with an incredibly sweet perfume floating on top. This led to the collection and production of otto of rose and the Persians were leaders in the field for hundreds of years. If you filled a wide-mouthed crock with water, completely covered the water with rose petals and let it stand outside overnight, in the morning, when you removed the petals, you would see a film of oil on the water. This is otto—but with such a tiny quantity, I'm hard put to tell you how it could be skimmed off and saved.

In roses, the scent lies primarily in the petal, and in the leaf of some varieties. Sometimes it is the root, as in vetiver, that contains the plant's perfume. Other plants keep their scents in the leaves, or in the barks, or in their gums and resins. Small, almost invisible pockets or vessels contain the volatile oils that form when the plant is mature. To extract scent we trap the component that carries the scent in a substance which can be easily added to the perfume.

❀

EXTRACTING ESSENTIAL OILS

As oil is attracted to oil, one of the most successful approaches to obtaining floral essences is to soak—or *macerate*—flowers in a pure oil. In France, fine perfume oils or pomades, as the solids are called, are obtained by macerating flowers in a mixture of pure suet and lard. An easier way is to use pure olive oil or safflower oil. Using a large mixing bowl or comparable vessel, pour in a quart of pure oil and put in as many fresh flowers as it will take. The flowers should be ones with sweet, strong fragrances: roses, lilacs, tuberoses, orange flowers.

Let the flowers soak for twelve to forty-eight hours, then remove them and add more fresh blossoms. You can either strain the oil into another bowl through cheesecloth or carefully lift out the flowers with a slotted spoon. Straining is best as you can squeeze all the oils from the wilted blossoms. This process should be repeated with at least ten batches of fresh flowers . . . or more if your garden will supply them. When you have finished macerating the flowers, strain the oil and bottle with a tight cap. You have now a pure oil of flowers to add to all kinds of perfumes.

When you purchase flower oils from a supplier, you should be getting a similar product, with perhaps a small percentage of alcohol added. Tincture, or extract, on the other hand, is primarily alcohol scented with a flower oil. Many perfume recipes call for tinctures: They are not difficult to make and you can do a number at a time if you have enough stoppered bottles.

MAKING TINCTURES

To prepare a tincture you need 90 to 96 percent pure rectified alcohol. This costs more than the rubbing variety but is odorless and colorless. Unfortunately, it is extremely hard to find. A bottle of vodka works almost as well. The approximate proportions are one part flower oil—either homemade or purchased—to ten parts alcohol. The tincture can be bottled and set aside for use.

Tinctures can also be made by chopping, grinding, or otherwise reducing solid materials to a fine state and soaking them in alcohol for a week or two. Before bottling, the tinctures are filtered through coffee filter paper and, if you want to make them perfectly clear, through powdered talc.

Here is a step-by-step procedure for making tincture of tonka beans: Chop or grind one part tonka beans and add to six parts alcohol. Cover the bottle with a washrag folded in four or some other porous, thick material, fasten with a rubber band, and store in a cool, dark place for one to two weeks. After the allotted time, pour the mixture through a coffee filter paper in which you have poured about four tablespoons of talc from the drugstore. This will purify the liquid and make it clear. Bottle and stopper. The proportions for some other fixative tinctures are as follows: powdered orris root, one part; alcohol, five parts; storax, one part; alcohol, 15 parts; benzoin, one part; alcohol, six parts.

To make citrus tincture, one of the most useful, grind, grate, or very finely slice about 24 sweet orange rinds and soak them in a quart of alcohol. Use a large enough bottle so the contents can be effectively shaken about. Shake daily. Strong fragrances such as cinnamon, cloves and vanilla can be made into tinctures in this way.

SCENTS BY DISTILLATION

With very delicate flowers such as jasmine and lily-of-the-valley, the best way to extract scents is by distillation. This requires either a homemade or hobby-shop still and the stove. There isn't much actual difference between the distilled essences and the ones obtained from macerating in alcohol, but this method captures the more delicate aromas far more faithfully. The essential oils contained in the flowers are released by a combination of heat and alcohol and carried in vapors to a clean vessel where they reform *as* liquid.

To make a still you will need a large jar, and a smaller one. Both must have tops with holes in them which will hold a piece of tubing. Either use a cork lid (which is easier to pierce) or a tight-fitting screw-on lid. Set the large jar in a pan of water on the stove. Place a length of copper tubing about one-third of the way down; pass the other end into the receiver jar which sits in a pan of cool water and is swathed in a damp towel.

Half-fill the "stove" jar with two quarts of distilled water, one of pure alcohol, and two quarts of flower blossoms. Make sure the tube clears the contents. Heat the pan of water, keeping an eye on the alcohol and water in the still: When it begins to barely move, reduce the heat, and keep the liquid at a constant, very low simmer. The steam that rises will carry with it most of the flowers' oils and a good bit of the alcohol as well as water. At the end of several

hours, you should have transferred about two-thirds of the liquid and extracted the best of what the flowers have to offer. Stop at this point. You now have a "water." A general rule is that from six pounds of fresh flower blossoms, you will realize a quart and a half of waters. You can work with smaller quantities if you prefer.

To make **Bouquet's Water,** a toilet water of delicious fragrance, distill together jasmine, lily, rose and orange flowers. To bring home a straying husband, according to Persian myth, put cinnamon, cloves and cardamoms in a glass jar. Over this read the Yaslin chapter of the Koran seven times—backwards. Then fill the jar up with rose water in which you have soaked one of your husband's shirts. In the shirt pocket there should be a piece of paper on which his name and the names of any four angels are written. Heat the jar. When it reaches a good boil, your husband should be on his way home to stay.

PART II

THE

RECIPES

POTPOURRI

Potpourri (Pō pŏo rē'—a mixture of dried flower petals and spices used to perfume) is a relatively new addition to our formal collection of perfumed products. The Egyptian kings who had enormous quantities of fresh roses placed in crocks and buried for later use were probably the first to experiment with what the French later designated "rotten pot"—potpourri. The old way to make potpourri, also called sweet jar, is by the moist method. The ingredients literally do rot. Today, we usually make it by the dry method.

The classic potpourri is composed largely of rose petals mixed with other flowers, roots, herbs, spices, woods and leaves and flavored with various oils. After being treated and seasoned, these mixtures are placed in ornamental jars, baskets and crocks and used to scent the room. Both dry and moist methods are successful and share many of the same advantages, but as there are differences in their preparation they will be discussed separately. Both can be made with the same ingredients so if one of the recipes appeals to you and the method doesn't, switch them around.

DRY POTPOURRI

Dry potpourri is prepared from dried materials, the bulk of which is traditionally rose petals. Besides the great appeal of its perfume, and the possible loveliness of its container—cut-glass, basketry or open-work silver—the potpourri itself has a subtle beauty. Its rose petals are a blend of hues from black-red to flesh, from soft magenta to pink, from clove-brown to chamois; its dried leaves range from deep olive to pale celadon greens; touches of color from other dried petals add soft blues, purples, oranges, yellows and white. In the dry potpourri, color is enhanced by pattern—intricately shaped leaves, crescent petals, tiny rosebuds, and delicate cobweb grass forms.

Although there are a few special exceptions, most dry potpourris appear muted and soft—almost all flowers dry with only a memory of their former brilliance. Even the names of some of the popular roses suggest gentleness: Peace, Pigeon's Throat, Dusty Rose, Suntan, Nymph's Thigh. Some of the very red roses dry almost black. The whites all fade to some shade of beige, usually not the most attractive one. Exceptions to the muted rose color are the family of orangy roses often tipped with yellow. The petals from these dry a brilliant red, almost day-glo color. Some of the yellows will dry with a bright color, too, as will a few of the stronger pinks.

If you can grow at least six rose bushes you can accumulate enough petals over the blooming season to make a number of potpourris and sachets. Or, you can buy the dried petals and rosebuds at a fairly reasonable cost from one of the herb houses or perfume suppliers. You can also save rose petals from flowers from the florist, but they are mostly used for bulk as their scent dissipates after the flower has passed full bloom.

Collect the flowers in the morning before the sun is high. They should be rid of all traces of early dew and each blossom should be just opened, at the peak of its bloom. This is the hardest part for me: I am torn between keeping the flowers for a few days either on the bush or in the house and preparing them at once. The longer they are kept, the less essential oil remains.

The flowers should be cut on a dry day, after a few days of clear weather. Pass over blooms that are rain-damaged. Cut the flowers from the bushes and gently pull the petals from them, discarding the other parts. A few perfect, small green leaves should be kept each time. Some of your roses will have fragrant leaves; they should be stripped from the stem and kept. Each time you gather petals, snip off a few small, tightly closed rosebuds for decoration. Carefully pull them whole from the stem and treat them gently so they will retain their form.

All flowers, and roses in particular, are best dried away from strong light and where the air can circulate around them. A well-ventilated attic or shady back porch is ideal. Some sort of drying rack is needed. The best racks are made from window screens. These can be supported on bricks or concrete blocks and, if you need more than one, can be stacked one on top of the other at least a foot apart. Newspaper on the floor in an out-of-the-way place can also be used but it doesn't work nearly as well as the screen which allows circulation of air on both surfaces of the petals. If your drying place is breezy, put a layer of cheesecloth over the petals to keep them from fluttering away.

The petals on racks must be stirred and turned every few days; those on paper, every day. Your goal is to have petals dried to the consistency of a cereal flake—dry crisp. This takes two days or more depending on the moisture in the batch of petals and the location of the drying racks. Be sure that the petals are only one deep. If you're in a hurry to dry the petals, they can be scattered on a cookie sheet and placed in a warm oven (about 110 degrees) with the door open to allow the moisture to escape. Shake them gently from time to time to make sure all are thoroughly exposed to the heat. They should be dry in less than an hour. Other flowers can be dried along with the petals using either method.

Small flowers such as violets and pansies that are needed for decoration alone should be dried between sheets of newspaper weighted with a heavy book to keep them flat. A Sunday supplement can hold hundreds of these little blooms between its pages. As flowers dry they lose about half their weight and bulk.

Have ready large glass containers such as pickle jars or earthenware crocks. The containers must have tight-fitting lids. As the petals dry, carefully place them in the container. Make sure not to break the petals. See to it that the container is securely closed. You can add new dried petals to this supply as the summer progresses. If you use a glass jar be sure it is placed in a dark pantry or wrapped with paper. Sunlight will leach the color from the already delicately hued petals. When thoroughly dry, the petals will remain just as placed in the jars for months.

After all this discussion about drying, about how careful one must be, how precise, I have to admit to some rather peculiar practices of my own during the time we were making potpourri commercially.

We were living in Arizona then where the normal humidity is so low that most flowers dried overnight. We imported many of our roses from California fields where the bushes were being grown for sale; the blossoms weren't used. In the middle of their growing season we received in a single shipment, by bus across the deserts, twenty-one enormous cartons of rose blossoms; each box weighed over one hundred pounds, making over a ton of flowers. Normally we dried flowers in mattress cartons and had over thirty of them on hand; but the first half-box from California filled them completely. We cleaned the floor of the double garage and began scattering petals over the cement floor. As we unpacked rose heads, it began to rain and the temperature dropped. For three days it rained while five of us frantically pulled petals. We hung the mattress boxes from the rafters, filled them, and kept tossing petals across the garage floor.

Meanwhile, the unopened boxes began smelling, as the roses, shut up in plastic bags, developed heat and fermented. The back of the house smelled as if a still was boiling away in the woods. In the garage, the petals piled up and, at the end of four days, the garage was knee-deep in red petals while the children, who missed fall leaves in the desert, made wild dives into the sweet red carpet. We futilely tossed the petals with grass rakes trying to encourage air circulation . . . and the rains poured down.

Some dried; those around the edges of the ocean of petals and those we'd put in the house, but the bulk slowly turned into brown sludge. The dry air returned and the sludge dried to a fine, brown powder, suitable for mulch around the fruit trees.

Our commercial venture ended shortly thereafter. I had mixed emotions about it; as pleasant as all of the materials were, mixing potpourri day after day in fifty-gallon cans would send me running for the vinegar with which I'd wash the perfume from my arms.

The following year we moved to a grove of avocados in south Florida where the humidity is always high. Soon after our arrival, we had the opportunity to manufacture a number of potpourri kits for one of the women's magazines. Of lavender and roses, we still had aplenty, gunny sacks full. We were surrounded by the most fragrant of all trees, lemon, lime, orange, grapefruit, and, most of all, rough or bitter lemon. And for sheer beauty, though without any scent, great climbers of bougainvillea, the bracts of which dry with their brilliant reds, pinks and oranges intact. But how to dry anything in south Florida in the summer? In the clothes dryer! Bougainvillea flowers in pillowcases on the "permanent press" cycle; sheaves of citrus leaves tossed in on "regular"; mint leaves and rosemary, basil and thyme from the garden dried in the children's room, the only airconditioning in the big, old house. And tiny slices of citrus went into the oven. Delightful potpourri!

But you'll never have to deal with such quantities so, as my mother often said, "Do as I say, not as I do."

When you have enough flowers to make the potpourri, ready your other ingredients. You will need a large bowl or a roasting pan or the top of a table covered with foil or waxed paper, one of the vegetable fixatives in ground form (for dry potpourri avoid anything powdered as it will cloud the container), spices, and whatever other dry material you find appealing. The fixative could be calamus root or sliced orris or storax. Generally, you will need a little more than a tablespoon for each quart of dried flowers. In approximately the same proportion, you will use one tablespoon of spice to a quart of petals. Add the spices you have chosen—cinnamon bark broken fine, rubbed mace, ground cardamom seeds, whatever—by sprinkling them over the petals and fixatives. Add the other dry ingredients you have selected: dried and crushed or fine-sliced citrus peel, rose leaves, some vetiver root, a small piece of crumbled vanilla bean. All should be absolutely dry. With your hands, gently and thoroughly mix the ingredients together.

If this is a first potpourri, now is the time to separate the dry ingredients into several batches and experiment with the oils and tinctures. You have a basic potpourri: To one batch, add a tincture of musk or amber; to another, a few drops of otto of rose and some rose geranium oil; to the third some neroli oil and perhaps a little more of the dried citrus peel. If you have herbs available, try rosemary with the animal-essence batch, mint with the neroli, and so on. Now is the time to experiment with the ingredients and combinations that will produce the most pleasing final fragrance.

When you are satisfied that the petals and other ingredients are sufficiently scented and mixed, place each batch in a separate container and close tightly. Leave enough room in the container so you can gently turn the crock and keep the elements well mixed. This aging process will take about six weeks to be perfect but it can be used after three weeks.

After a week or so you can open the crocks and evaluate the fragrances. This is difficult at first as the mixtures will

have a raw smell until they are properly aged and blended, but you can get some idea of what the end product will be. You can add a few more drops of the oils or a little more spice, depending on your sense of smell. If more petals come dry during the process, these can be added but keep in mind the proportions of fixatives necessary to hold scents.

After the dried ingredients are well blended you will come to what to me is the best part—selecting a container. It's all a pleasure, the gathering and drying, the mixing and blending, but this final step requires imagination and taste.

In selecting a container for dry potpourri, keep two things in mind: First, you have something with a delicious fragrance that needs to escape into the air to perfume your rooms; second, your potpourri has considerable beauty and you will want it to be partly visible.

Perhaps the most practical containers to hold scent for a long time are the old-fashioned glass candy or apothecary jars—the kind that sometimes hold fancy soaps. The ones with straight sides and lids are the easiest to work with as you can get your fingers inside to decorate the walls of the jar. The lid can remain on until you want the perfume to do its sweet work.

If you select glass jars, beat up the white of an egg and use this invisible glue to attach decorations to the sides of the container. Moisten your finger with the eggwhite and put a little dot of it on the inside of the jar. Then press on a small, dried violet, a pansy, a tiny leaf or whatever decorative bit you like. This can be done in as many places as you like. When you begin thinking potpourri, you will discover a new feeling for all sorts of little odd-shaped flower parts, leaves and stems. Dry them carefully and set them aside for decoration.

When you have finished decorating the jars, turn the

potpourri out onto a table or pan, being careful to avoid breakage, and mix well. Be sure that the fixatives are well dispersed; don't let them clump in one place or the other elements will quickly lose their scent. Carefully ladle the potpourri into the jars, filling them almost to the top.

I like using the glass and tin boxes available from Mexico; they come in interesting sizes and shapes and have straight sides. With this kind of container, you can fill it to capacity with potpourri and decorate afterwards. Take a tableknife, slip it down between the potpourri and the glass side, and insert your decorative flowers as you hold back the mass with the knife. When you remove the knife, the potpourri holds the decorative piece quite tightly.

If you can find them, old cut-glass or crystal jars make beautiful containers. Their facets pick up and abstract the delicate colors and shapes of the flowers and leaves.

Another way to show off your flowers is to use small baskets about nine inches across. Buy some pale green netting and cut it in 20-inch rounds. Lay the net on the table and, starting at the center, cover an area the size of the top of the basket with decorative leaves, buds and other forms. Put the best colored petals on the bottom followed by the bulk of the dry mixture. Draw the net up over the potpourri—there should be enough to fill the basket to its top—then gather and tie it off so that it forms a ball. This gathered part is attached to the bottom of the basket with the decorated side facing up.

Now you will have a basketful of sweet-scented flowers the top of which is decorated with little bits that give it color and form. Experiment with spidery stems and baby's breath, a tiny trio of rosebuds tied together, a little group of grass blades, a sliver or two of finely cut lemon or orange peel. You may choose to tie a pale green or rose-colored velvet ribbon around the rim of the basket. Or bring a ribbon over the edge and tie it with a small, flat bow. The more you play with your creations, the more ideas you will get. They make the nicest presents.

The baskets will not retain their scents as long as the covered jars; you have to decide what is most desirable, appearance or longevity. If the potpourri becomes dry smelling after a few months, add a tablespoon of French brandy to reactivate the perfumes. An open mixture that is well mixed and scented will last from one season to the next. One that is tightly closed most of the day should last for several years—longer if you add oils and brandy from time to time.

Another lovely container for dry potpourri is an old, open-work silver candy or fruit basket. During the Victorian era much ornate silver was made and if you have or can get one of these fanciful little baskets at an antique shop it can be treated like the straw basket. Any small, decorative silver piece with enough open space to display your mixture can be used. You may want to substitute a pale silver net for this, as the colors of potpourri in silver are particularly subtle and soft.

Although roses comprise most potpourris, it is possible to use other flowers, especially if you have access to other growing things or want a basket of a more colorful mixture. You might buy the little white ceramic "woven" baskets sold at variety stores and fill them with a mixture of red cardinal flowers, beebalm, and Paul's scarlet, and blue delphinium, larkspur, bachelor's buttons and cornflowers. For white add daisy and baby's breath. These flowers have little scent but with the addition of good fixatives and essential oils, you can make a fragrant, colorful potpourri.

If you prefer combinations of red and orange and yellow, use tiger lily, yellow primrose, nasturtium and marigold. Asters, particularly the purples, make a nice effect when taken apart. Hollyhock and broom keep their color. Keep your eyes open when you're in the country and try bits of whatever you can find. Just pick one flower and hang it in a dark place for a few days. Even flowers that dry without color can be used for bulk under roses. Note: It takes about two ounces of dry mixture for a small potpourri and about three pounds to fill an old umbrella stand. Most potpourris are made with one to three ounces of dried materials.

Here are some recipes for dry potpourris. Follow the general directions described earlier. If you cannot find some of the ingredients substitute another material from the same fragrance family. All recipes are in dry weight unless otherwise noted.

ROSE-LAVENDER POTPOURRI

Start with 10 ounces each of rose petals and lavender and add five ounces of sweet rose leaves and two ounces of ground orris root. Combine with three-quarters of an ounce of cinnamon bark broken fine, one-half ounce each of allspice and clove, and six drops of oil of tonka bean or 10 beans ground.

BAY-ROSE POTPOURRI

This calls for a quantity of rose petals; if you've not got this amount, cut it accordingly, remembering the general rule of one tablespoon of fixative to a quart of rose petals plus a tablespoon of spice.

To three quarts of rose petals add 12 torn bay leaves, two handfuls of lavender flowers, and one handful each of orange blossoms, violets and clove carnations. Mix in two ounces of orris root, one ounce of pounded-up nutmeg, one-fourth ounce each of cinnamon and ground clove, and sprinkle with one-half ounce of oil of neroli.

From a lovely book on herbs by Rosetta Clarkson, *Herbs, Their Culture and Uses,* here are two of the author's favorites:

SPICE POTPOURRI I

Mix one quart of rose petals with one-half pint of lavender flowers, a teaspoon of anise seed, one tablespoon of cloves, nutmeg and cinnamon mixed together and crushed, one tablespoon of crushed benzoin, and five drops each of oils of jasmine, rose geranium, patchouli and rosemary.

SPICE POTPOURRI II

Combine one quart of rose petals with a heaping tablespoon of crushed cinnamon, nutmeg, allspice, mace and cloves (ground together but not powdered). Add one heaping tablespoon of dried and ground orange peel, three drops of eucalyptus oil, five drops of peppermint oil, and one tablespoon of lavender flowers.

Caswell-Massey is a very old drugstore in New York City that stocks many of the elements you will need for making perfumes—as well as a delightful line of fresh fruit-based cosmetics—all presented in a Victorian-style catalogue. In it, Mr. Massey, one of the original owners, gives this recipe for his favorite potpourri.

MR. MASSEY'S FAVORITE POTPOURRI

To four ounces each of coriander, orris root, and rose petals, add two ounces of lavender flowers, one-half ounce of cinnamon, one-half ounce of mace, one-fourth ounce each of cloves, table salt, oils of lavender, cinnamon, clove, and rose, and one-half ounce of tincture of musk.

His partner, Mr. Caswell, preferred this variation:

MR. CASWELL'S FAVORITE POTPOURRI

Combine eight ounces each of lavender flowers, rose petals, and orris root with four ounces of table salt, two ounces each of clove, cinnamon, benzoin, and allspice,

three ounces of crushed tonka bean, and one-eighth ounce each of oils of lavender, sandalwood, rose geranium, rose, and bergamot. Add one-fourth ounce of oil of lemon and one-half ounce each of tinctures of musk and amber.

This is an extremely fragrant mixture and the addition of the animal essences and lemon oil give it a fruity note. It's one of my favorite combinations—fresh and sexy with a "young" bouquet.

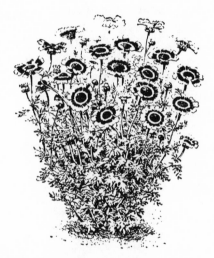

INDIAN POTPOURRI

This mixture uses patchouli, the mysterious Indian scent. To some, patchouli has an attic smell. This combination doesn't—it's strange but quite appealing and is made without rose petals.

Mix one ounce each of ground orris root and ground tonka bean, two ounces of ground santal (or sandalwood if necessary), one-half ounce of oakmoss (or one of the other mosses if not available), two ounces of orange leaves, and six ounces of lavender flowers. Add from one to three ounces of oil of patchouli or six ounces of the flower, if available. Modify according to your taste. Adding a little ground cinnamon tends to calm down the patchouli.

LAVENDERWOOD POTPOURRI

This has an old-fashioned, delicate fragrance: Use 16 ounces of lavender flowers combined with two ounces of sweet woodruff, one and one-half ounces each of moss and thyme, eight ounces of slivered orange peel, four ounces of benzoin, and several handfuls of other available flowers—cornflowers, peppermint flowers and violets are appropriate to the scent. Finish off with one-fourth ounce of clove and anise combined. This mixture makes a particularly nice sachet as well.

ROSEMARY POTPOURRI

To one quart of rose petals add two pints of crushed lemon verbena leaves, one pint of rose geranium leaves, and one of rosemary slightly crushed, a tablespoon of dried and crushed orange peel, two tablespoons of benzoin and orris mixed, a small quantity of finely cut angelica root (an herb of the carrot family), and a small quantity of mixed cinnamon, nutmeg, and sliced ginger root (available at oriental food shops). Over this mixture sprinkle six drops each of oils of tonka, rosemary and neroli.

HUNGARIAN POTPOURRI

Here is another with rosemary as an important ingredient: Start with four ounces of the fragrant leaf, and add two ounces each of orange blossoms and mint leaves, two ounces each of calamus and vetiver crushed, and three ounces each of rose petals and dried, ground lemon peel. If you have it (or have made it) sprinkle on a little eau-de-cologne; it will make the rosemary scent stronger and sweeter.

PEPPERMINT POTPOURRI

Here is a sixteenth-century recipe from Mrs. Clarkson's book: To one pint each of peppermint leaves, thyme, and lavender flowers, add one tablespoon of crushed coriander, cloves, and nutmeg combined, two tablespoons of crushed caraway seeds, and a tablespoon of crushed benzoin.

JASMINE POTPOURRI

This has a lovely, sultry perfume: To eight ounces of jasmine flowers add four ounces each of calamus, geranium leaves and orange blossoms. Mix in two ounces each of cassia and benzoin sprinkled with one ounce of oil of vanilla. You'll think you're way down South.

CHYPRE POTPOURRI

Patchouli used to be the signature for all chypre scents but, gradually, the dry, sweet mosses took them over: To

eight ounces of orange blossoms add four ounces of oakmoss, two ounces each of rose petals, benzoin, bitter al-
monds (or one-half ounce of the oil) and santal. Moisten
with a few drops of oil of lemon or lime.

MOIST POTPOURRI

This old way to make potpourri is still a good one. You
don't have to be as careful handling the materials and,
more importantly, the scent has greater staying power.
Some moist potpourris are said to retain their perfumes for
as long as fifty years. I find a difference in the quality of the
moist scent as well; it is usually a bit heavier regardless of
the ingredients.

Another plus for the moist method is that you can use a
really wide range of pots and jars. One possibility is a small
china jar with two covers: One is solid, the other (underneath) has holes through which the perfume escapes into
the room.

There are many lovely oriental jars that are suitable for
this mixture. A friend has one that came from China in the
early 1800s: it stands about three feet high and contains an

old, lightly scented, fruity concoction. When the cover is removed the entire room is filled with a delicious, subtle perfume. You can use anything that is not transparent, from china marmalade crocks to the finest porcelain.

To make moist potpourris, pick the flowers as you would for the dry: early in the day when they are dry, after several days of dry weather and just as the flowers come to full bloom. They need some drying after picking, either on the screens, on papers or in the oven. What you want is a soft, leathery texture, not crisp, just very limp with about one-third of their bulk gone.

You will need a large widemouthed, straight-sided crock with a tight cover and a long wooden spoon. This mixture needs to be stirred as it matures; the size and shape of the crock should make it easy to mix and should hold all the petals you plan to accumulate for this potpourri. The moist mixture matures in this crock for at least two weeks. In olden days, ladies of leisure left these crocks a-stewing for months at a time; evidently, the longer they age, the longer the scent will last. But we aren't that patient anymore.

Floral Clock.

Into the crock pour a layer of rose petals or other half-dried flowers and cover it with a layer of common (non-iodized) salt. Continue to alternate layers of petals and salt until the crock is about three-quarters full—or you have exhausted your supply of petals. You can add more flowers throughout the summer, but each batch needs at least ten days to mature.

Something heavy will be needed to press the mass down: A plate weighted down with a flat iron or a heavy jar of fruit can be used. Make sure this object is easy to lift because each day the container must be opened and stirred well from the bottom. If a sort of broth forms, mix it in with the petals. Sometimes a hard cake will appear after a few weeks. This should be taken out, crushed and added to the other ingredients during the final mixing.

There are two ways to make this potpourri: You can either get a large quantity of petals together and add the spices, oils and other perfuming ingredients at one time—or you can mature the flowers and when the aging is finished, take them out and complete the recipe. The easiest way, of course, is to do it all at once.

Estimate the quantity of petals you will have and pick your recipe. Measure out and stir in the spices and leaves, roots and fixatives, and let them blend during the next month. When you are a week or so away from removing the mass, scent it with the right amounts of essential oils and tinctures. Let this all stew, stirring every day. Then pour the whole into a large mixing bowl and bolster with more oils as needed. The potpourri can then be thoroughly mixed and ladled into the containers you have selected. It will smell a little raw for a few weeks, but as it matures, the fragrances will mellow.

The following are recipes for moist potpourri; the ingredients listed for the dry method can be substituted.

BROWN SUGAR POTPOURRI

Take two gallons of partially dried rose petals and alternate in a crock with layers of salt (or bay salt, which is described below). Measure the salt to be used and make up an equal quantity of a mixture of allspice, cloves and brown sugar, one-quarter pound of gum benzoin, and two ounces of crushed orris root. This goes in with the salt layers. Add one-quarter pint of brandy and any sort of fragrant flowers you have on hand. Citrus leaves, lemon verbena and rose geranium leaves can also be added. Make sure they have all been partially dried first. Allow this mixture to age for a month, stirring every day. Once it has matured, turn it out into a large pan, mix thoroughly, and fill about four good-sized containers. This is an old recipe and is said to retain its perfume for at least 50 years with the occasional addition of some French brandy.

Bay salt is called for in a number of recipes. Take common (non-iodized) salt and to about a pound, add six torn bay leaves. With a wooden spoon, or mortar and pestle, crush the salt over the leaves until the leaves are exhausted. The salt picks up a slightly bay scent which is pleasant.

This next recipe also requires a large quantity of rose petals, but like Brown Sugar Potpourri, it can easily be cut down to fit your supply. Although the ingredients should be kept more or less in proportion when you change any of the mixtures, there is an almost consistent *inconsistency* in the strength and floral overtones of the various brands of oils and tinctures, and the flowers and spices you buy and grow. An eighth ounce in or out isn't going to make a criti-

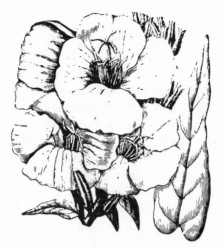

cal difference—except with animal essences. These concoctions are made mostly "by nose."

EARLY SPRING POTPOURRI

To one basket of rose petals and buds add a handful each of orange flowers, violets and jasmine, one-half ounce sliced or ground or powdered orris root, one-half ounce cinnamon, one-quarter ounce tincture of musk, one-quarter pound sliced or ground angelica root, a small handful of ground cloves, and one handful each of rosemary, bay laurel leaves, peppermint, balm and bergamot leaves. Prepare and add two ground clove-stuck oranges (a description follows). Pour in a small bottle—about an ounce—of extract of New Mown Hay and moisten the mixture with a jigger of brandy. This entire combination is alternated with salt in the crock, stirred every day for a month, and turned out into containers.

Orange and clove are combined in this manner: Take sweet oranges, cut in quarters, scrape out the pulp completely with a spoon, and stick the peel with cloves. Place these in a warm oven and allow to dry completely. When removed from the oven, the peels will be hard and crisp. Place then in a mortar or wooden bowl and pound into a powder. This scent alone is delicious and closely matches that of pomander balls described later in the book.

Brandy is called for in many recipes, too. It is used to revive tired sachets and potpourris as the alcohol releases the latent scent molecules in the dry materials. For many thousands of years only oils were used to make perfumes, the ancients having no notion of alcohol's ability to dissolve and release aromatics. Wine was the first solvent; now we use brandy, a few drops for an old sachet, a tablespoon for a weak potpourri.

MILLEFLEUR POTPOURRI

Here's one I like because you can use anything that looks appealing. Get in the habit of making frequent stops by the roadside and picking all kinds of flowers. If you want to make a moist potpourri, partially dry whatever you have found and put it aside in a covered jar. The petals will retain some moisture and by the time you have all you need, the early batches can be brought out and used. Perhaps this recipe should be named *Roadside*.

Collect about four quarts of any combination of flowers and leaves. Mix them in a large pan with the finely cut and sun- or air-dried peelings of two lemons, one ounce each of powdered orris root, gum benzoin, cinnamon and nutmeg, all crushed. Add 12 bay leaves, a few sage, rosemary and lavender leaves, and moisten the whole with one-quarter ounce tincture of musk, one ounce of lavender water, one ounce of bergamot oil, and one of eau-de-cologne. Mix this well, layer it in a crock with bay salt, and allow it to age for a month or longer.

Here are several recipes with fewer ingredients and in smaller quantities:

ORANGE-MINT POTPOURRI

To eight ounces of orange flowers add four ounces of mint leaves (white mint is best), three ounces of coriander seeds, well crushed, one ounce each of benzoin and oakmoss, two ounces each of ground vetiver and calamus root. The orange flowers should be fresh or only partly wilted when put in the crock, and the mixture should be alternated with layers of salt which has been ground with rosemary.

VIOLET POTPOURRI

This has no violets in it, of course, as dry they have no scent, but no one could ever tell: To eight ounces of ground orris root add four ounces of dried rose leaves, two ounces of benzoin, two ounces of ground tonka bean, four of mint leaves, one-eighth ounce of bitter almond, and one-quarter ounce of violet oil. Mix and alternate with salt in the crock.

The only difficult thing about making any of these pot-pourris and the following sachets is to learn to gauge what you are smelling and take into account initial rawness. When flowers first begin to dry they have a delicious scent; halfway through, they smell as if they should be thrown away. Only after they are mixed, fixed and matured does the original floral odor return. When the raw odor is uppermost, there is a tendency to over-perfume with oils because it doesn't seem possible such a musty, unpleasant dead-flower scent will ever amount to anything. Have faith. Hidden away is perfume for the future.

SACHET

Sachet (Sa shā'—a small bag containing perfumed powder used to scent clothes) is the most fragrant way in the world to perfume clothes, linens and note papers. Victorian ladies sewed little sachets into, and attached them onto, everything in the house from arm chairs to sewing baskets. You can sprinkle bits of sachet in the envelopes of personal mail, hang bags in clothes closets, lay little pouches with your lingerie, make embroidered envelopes to place in gifts of handkerchiefs and blouses or even tuck some bags among the sofa pillows.

Bags for sachet are sewn from small bits of silk. For more elaborate designs, a less tightly woven fabric can be used over the silk, but silk or an equally tight weave must hold the sachet as it tends to powder and would otherwise leak. Depending on their use, sachets can range in size and shape from tiny, plump pillows of two inches square to envelope-size, flat pouches to lay in drawers between clothes. They can be tied up in fat purses with ribbons to hang in the closet. If you like needlework, they are delightful, small canvases for your most elaborate flights of fancy. The nicest sachet I ever saw was in the rural South. An elderly lady had gathered jasmine and roses and things from her truck garden and just made a "mess" of flowers and roots to hang over the front door of what could only be called a shack. It was ill-made and lumpy, its covering was a piece of printed cotton flour sacking, but it smelled like heaven.

To make sachet you dry the ingredients as you would for dry potpourri. All petals and leaves must be quite crisp, otherwise they may mildew. You can make sachet from dry potpourris or you can start from scratch with small quantities of flower materials. For novices, sachet is probably the easiest perfume product as it requires an absolute minimum of ingredients. If you concoct a sachet that is particularly pleasing, you can apply its recipe to larger, whole-flower quantities for dry potpourris . . . or using the moist method, work in that area.

As even a good-sized sachet won't call for much more than one ounce of dried mixture, you can easily estimate what you need to pick, find and buy. After drying and mixing with other ingredients, the sachet should be crumbled to just this side of powder; roots and barks and such must be well ground and a mortar and pestle are almost essential for things like cinnamon bark and seeds. The mixed ingredients are placed in covered jars to age for about two weeks and should be stirred every day. A few drops of one of the animal tinctures will help hold the scent in this continuously open perfume product.

PATCHOULI SACHET

Mix together eight ounces each of vetiver root, rose leaves or rose geranium leaves, six ounces of patchouli leaves, and five ounces of ground mace. This scent goes well with woolen clothes and blankets.

WINTER SACHET

This is the best one for furs and wools: To one-half pound of dried rosemary add the same of mint leaves, four ounces of thyme, and two tablespoons of ground cloves. Mix this well and age it and make larger sachets to scent your summer storage. No moth will go near it. It will keep animals from chewing naturally cured Indian rugs if a bit is sprinkled on them.

FLORIDA SACHET

To eight ounces of orange flowers add three ounces of ground coriander seeds, four ounces of fresh or six ounces of dried mint leaves, one ounce of benzoin, two ounces of vetiver root, two ounces of calamus, and one ounce of oakmoss. Sprinkle with four drops of neroli oil and let it age, checking from time to time to see if it's fruity enough.

OAKASIA SACHET

Oakmoss has a light, heady aroma which can serve as the basis for many pleasant sachets. When you add dried acacia flowers, it's delightful: Combine two ounces each of oakmoss, santal or ground sandalwood (white), and two ounces of orris root. To this add one ounce of ground tonka bean or four drops of oil of tonka, two ounces of dried and ground lemon peel, and four ounces of acacia flowers.

Combinations of ingredients that include oakmoss are often called chypre. The moss has come to replace the original chypre scent which was based on patchouli. If you can't get oakmoss and would like to try one of these scents, order oil of chypre.

ORANGE-ROSE SACHET

To eight ounces each of orange and rose blossoms add two ounces each of magnolia flowers and bitter orange peel finely ground. You may have to substitute two drops of magnolia oil. Add four ounces of fine-ground santal or sandalwood and moisten with four drops of oil of vanilla . . . not the cooking extract, ever . . . and a small vanilla bean crumbled fine.

SWEET BAG FOR LINEN

Here is what is believed to be the oldest recipe for sachet printed in America. It comes from a Colonial Williamsburg book, *The Compleat Housewife*, published in 1742:

"Take a Pound of orris-roots, a Pound of sweet Calamus, a Pound of Cypress-roots, a Pound of dried Lemon-peel, a Pound of dried Orange-peel, a Pound of dried Roses, make all these into a gross powder: Coriander-seeds four Ounces, Nutmegs one Ounce and half, an Ounce of Cloves: make all these into fine powder, and mix with the other: add musk and ambergrease: then take four large Handfuls Lavender flowers dried and rub'd, a Handful of sweet-Marjoram, a Handful of Orange-leaves, a Handful of young Walnut leaves, all dry'd and rub'd: mix all together with some bits of cotton perfumed with Essenses and put it up into silk Bags to lay with your Linen."

This would make enormous quantities of sachet! You will have noticed that the quantities of animal and flower essences aren't given. I suppose this was to be left to the perfumer's discretion—as it must be.

SACHET BASE

You can make this base and add oils to it as you like. It has a sweet, relatively "neutral" scent: To four ounces of powdered orris root add four ounces of ground sandalwood, one ounce of ground cedar, and one ounce of lavender flowers. Mix in one and one-half ounces each of sweet rose leaves and patchouli leaves, one ounce each of vetiver and amberette seed ground, one-third ounce of ground tonka bean and two-thirds ounce of benzoin, and a teaspoon of ground cloves. Sprinkle over this one-quarter ounce of tincture of musk. The entire mixture should be ground together into a fine powder and stored for two weeks in a crock. This can be scented with almost any oil.

LAVENDER SACHET

To six parts of the base add three parts of lavender flowers and some lavender oil to your "taste."

HELIOTROPE SACHET

Add 10 drops of heliotrope oil to the sachet base. This can be done with any number of oils from hyacinth to narcissus to Russian Leather.

As a good sachet can be made from such small quantities, try it with whatever you have on hand—a dozen roses, rosemary and mint from the grocer, a few wild flowers, the moss and orris and essential oils from the drugstore or supply house. Many boutiques and "psychedelic" stores carry oils. Apartment dwellers can grow the rose geraniums and perhaps a miniature citrus along with a few of the mints and herbs. You will be surprised at the number of materials you already have on hand that can be used to make these fragrant little bags.

You can even make sachet without flowers. Ground orris root or, cheaper and almost as good, rice flour or one of the mosses washed and dried and powdered will make the base. Combine equal parts of rice flour and powdered orris and add to them whatever oils you please. If you make or have a perfume you like, it can be used to scent this mixture—add one-eighth ounce of perfume to an ounce of the powdered mixture.

VERBENA SACHET

Mix one pound of dried and ground lemon peel, one-eighth ounce of oil of lemon grass, one-half ounce of oil of lemon peel, and one ounce of oil of bergamot mixed into one pound of orris root. Aged, this makes a delightful lemony sachet.

Once you begin experimenting with fresh, natural flower scents, you'll be amazed at the difference it makes in your general sense of well-being. The artificial sprays and solids will lose their appeal to the refreshing fragrance of the outdoors, of summer all year long.

BATH
POTPOURRI

Bath potpourri can be made from dry potpourri and sachet mixtures. All you need add is some borax. This is available on the grocer's shelf, just plain, old Twenty Mule Team. Mix equal parts of the borax and the sachet or potpourri mixture. Put this in a tightly covered jar and let it blend for about two weeks. Tie a teaspoon of this in a small purse of silk and hang it from the hot water tap as the bath runs. The steam releases the fragrance and gently scents you as you bathe.

One of the best scents for a bath concoction is the Florida Sachet (page 94). Add from a few drops to several ounces of oil of lemon—depending on how much mixture you want to make. It's like bathing in a lemon grove.

According to an old tale, a woman could find out if she'd have the man she wanted by carrying lemon peels in her pockets all through a day. That night, after rubbing the bedposts with the peelings, if she dreamed that the man handed her two lemons, she was sure to snare him. You might try the following recipe instead: Combine some rose petals, lavender flowers, ground orris root, ground-up stick cinnamon and a few drops of oil of clover. Mix with equal parts of borax, age for a week and tie in purses.

I sometimes use nylon purses with drawstrings and I refill them when they are used up. Make at least a dozen for gifts. You'll get many requests for more.

TOILET
WATERS

These are mostly old recipes—toilet waters were once popular. Try them, they are very delicate.

FLORIDA WATER

This is still a big seller: Take four pints of pure alcohol and add to it one-half pint of rose water, one ounce of tincture of musk, three ounces of tincture (or one ounce oil) of jasmine, one-half ounce each of oils of lemon and lavender, three drops of oil of neroli, four drops oil of cloves, one-eighth ounce oil of cinnamon, and one and one-half ounces oil of bergamot. Filter and set aside a month before using.

LAVENDER WATER

This is how "ladies" smelled when I was a child: To three pints of pure alcohol add one and one-quarter ounces of lavender oil, three-quarters ounce of oil of bergamot, three-quarters ounce of tincture of ambergris. Mix this thoroughly and bottle. If you want a really fine lavender water, try to get Mitchem or English lavender oil. This lavender water is also a nice base with which to experiment with other oils. Try a little tincture or oil of tonka, of angelica or of rosemary and see what you get.

Aging is necessary for all perfumes. Bottle and place in a dark room and "disturb" every few days. This does away with the same kind of raw smell unaged potpourri has.

GERANIUM WATER

To two pints of pure alcohol add four ounces of rose water, five drops tincture of musk, one ounce tincture of orris root, and one ounce of geranium oil and allow to age.

ROSE WATER

Here's an alternative to making rose water by distillation: Boil two quarts of distilled water and remove from the stove. Add one-eighth ounce of rose oil, four drops of oil of clove, and one pint of alcohol. Let this stand several days *before* bottling.

VIOLET WATER

To 20 ounces of alcohol add two ounces of violet extract, one ounce of cassia extract, one-half ounce of rose oil, and one-half ounce of tincture of orris root. Let this stand several days and add two pints of distilled water, shake well, filter and bottle.

The real difference between the "waters" and what we think of as perfume is that these are lighter, less complex of mixture, less persistent perhaps. But for a summer day, for a closed room, for a stroll in the sun, nothing is nicer.

INCENSE

Our first perfumes were, doubtless, the incense from the burning of sweet woods and resins. The word perfume comes from the Latin, *per*, through, and *fume*, smoke: from the Greek *thymos*, smoke or spirit. Through the fragrant smokes of ancient fires, gods were worshipped and the odor of burning sacrifices concealed. As civilizations formed, the central meeting place in small cities became the outdoor altar on which priests burned offerings to perfume the air. Ancient Egyptians burned substances to the sun god, Ra, on his daily journey across the heavens: Resin was used as he rose, myrrh when he was directly overhead, and a mixture of sixteen ingredients as he set in the evening. The use of incense is depicted in carvings and fragments of paintings from Babylon and formulas for its manufacture given in the Bible, and by Plutarch and the Greek physician, Galen.

For thousands of years the priests were also "doctors"

and it is probable that many of their clues for medications
came from experiments with new substances to use in tem-
ple offerings. Possibly, intoxicating herbs and plants such
as hemp were first ignited without foreknowledge of their
intoxicating properties. Galen said that the fumes of hashish, "the trembling," when inhaled, eased the muscles and
limbs and "what flows" and added that it ". . . produced
senseless talk." A Medieval Persian recipe for inducing
sleep was the inhalation of the smoke given off by the root
of mallow, "a salted, shrunken fish, the anterior end," and
morning-glory seeds. The fumes of a burning "puff-ball," a
mushroomlike plant, were said to be a well-recognized
narcotic.

As the human race expanded and became expert at city

building, great fires of woods and herbs were ignited to help ward off the plagues that regularly decimated their populations. And as sweet aromas were offered up to the gods, so were noxious ones used to keep devils away—and by some logic, to call them up. Pleasant fragrances were part of good, or "white" magic and old books on the supernatural give hundreds of recipes and rituals for invoking the proper spirits.

One ritual was to add incense oils to a shallow pan in which alcohol had been poured. This was placed in the middle of a room and set on fire. The participant locked his thumbs together and holding his hands over the burning pan shouted, "Tetragrammaton." This word incorporated all four Hebrew consonants of the name of God which, anciently, was not to be spoken aloud. If dry incense was used, "Tetragrammaton" had to be shouted seven times.

But it was left to the Orient to turn the use of incense into an art form—one which had a practical side. In a time of great drought thousands of years ago, the Chinese, who used clocks run by water, developed a method of telling time by incense. They designed open-work seals of metal which were placed on carefully tamped beds of ashes. Into the trenches of the seals they poured incense. When the seals were removed the incense lay in an intricate pattern with marks designating the hours. As the incense burned, one had but to look and observe its progress to tell the time of day. Elaborate boxes were designed to hold the "clocks" so capricious drafts wouldn't interfere with their function.

The Chinese also used a coil of incense with hourly markings. Later, the Japanese added a refinement. They divided the incense into different fragrances so the day would have an appropriate aroma for each of its moods. So accurate were these "Joss" sticks that Geishas said they had worked "three sticks," or however long their day had been.

The Japanese have a legend that burning incense calls up the Jiki-ko-ki who come to eat the smoke. In life, these spirits were men who made and sold bad incense and through eternity smoke is their only food. Until very recent years, various aromatic substances were burned in sickrooms and hospitals where they were thought to assist oxidation and ventilation, to neutralize the effects of some bacteria and to prevent the growth of others.

Today, we use incense to mitigate what the poet Shelley a hundred years ago called, "a time of smells and stenches"—in general to make life a little more pleasant.

Incense can be made in the form of oils to sprinkle on a fire or heat, in powder to warm in tiny braziers, in small cones and sticks to ignite, and ribbons and papers to burn. Whatever its form, heat is an integral part and some substance to encourage burning must be present. Also needed is something to hold the powdered ingredients together.

Gum tragacanth and **gum arabic** or **acacia gum** are the two principal glues used to hold powdered ingredients. Tragacanth "bleeds" from an Eastern tree in lovely shell-shaped translucent tears. When ground and soaked in water, it forms a paste that has many uses in industry. Tragacanth absorbs enormous quantities of water: An ounce will take up as much as a gallon in a week. Start with a tablespoon of powdered tragacanth to a large glass of water—do this in an old can. If need be, correct the consistency—you want a heavy paste that can be molded with the hands. Keep it well covered so it will remain soft. If tragacanth or the gum arabic pastes become hard before you work them, they can be softened in a double boiler with gentle heat and constant stirring.

Gum arabic absorbs less water but is treated in the same way. Both of these gums used to be available at the drugstore, but now you will probably have to ask the druggist to order them from a wholesaler. Experiment with either gum until you're happy with the consistency. When the oils and other powdered ingredients are added, it should form a manageable dough.

Saltpeter (sodium nitrate) ensures an even burn in powders, papers, solids, and such and is also obtainable from the druggist. It is either added to incense preparations in solution with water or used to soak the charcoal which is used for burning incense.

Sodium chlorate can't be purchased but it is used to treat the *self-igniting* charcoals you buy. This charcoal comes in pre-formed little cups in which you can burn powders and lumps of resin. You can also crush these cups to add to recipes that call for ground charcoal *and* saltpeter. Where recipes call for charcoal, you can use the commercial kind well ground up and soaked with saltpeter—or as the recipe suggests.

SOLID INCENSE—BASIC RECIPE

Take six ounces of charcoal, grind it up, and add one ounce of powdered benzoin, one-half ounce of saltpeter, one-quarter ounce of balsam of Tolu, one-quarter ounce of ground sandalwood and enough mucilage of tragacanth (or gum arabic) to make a stiff paste. The solid ingredients are ground to a fine powder and mixed into the tragacanth. After the addition of the scented oils, this is divided and rolled into small cones or thin rolls.

A cone-shaped mold is handy to use as it's hard to get an exact shape just with your fingers—but not impossible. You have to work quite fast and keep the unused portion in a bowl covered with a damp cloth. Set these little shapes aside to dry—which takes a day—and they're ready to ignite.

To make some self-igniting charcoal to use for incense, grind 30 ounces of charcoal and soak it in 30 ounces of water in which one-half ounce of saltpeter has been dissolved. Mix the charcoal-and-water solution thoroughly and set aside to dry.

There isn't much scent to these gluey mixtures; here's how to perfume them:

WOODY INCENSE

Men like these "natural" fragrances and they're lovely to throw on the cooking fire after you've finished with the business part of dinner: To 10 ounces of the basic mixture add one ounce of ground frankincense, one-half ounce of ground cloves, six drops tincture of musk, four drops each of oil of cinnamon, oil of Russian Leather, and juniper, and a small quantity of ground lavender flowers.

SUMMER INCENSE

Here's another for outdoors. You can either make it solid or leave the tragacanth out and use it as powder to toss on the embers: To each 10 ounces of the basic formula add one ounce each of powdered sandalwood, benzoin and orris, one-half ounce each of ground cardamom seeds and tincture of musk. Add four drops each of bergamot oil, neroli and cassaa oils. You can put some green food coloring in the water with the tragacanth to make green cones or sticks.

ROSEWOOD INCENSE

For a more sweetly perfumed incense, redolent of rose, add to 10 ounces of the basic recipe one-half ounce of oil of rose, one-eighth ounce tincture of civet, one-quarter ounce oil of bergamot, four drops of cinnamon oil, and one-quarter ounce oil of strawberry.

As you can see, you can play around endlessly with the fragrances—as long as you stay with compatible scents and keep the proportions fairly accurate.

CHURCH INCENSE

The incense used in churches has lots of frankincense; it has a heavy, penetrating odor: Grind up four ounces of frankincense and two ounces of myrrh and add a little oil of bergamot or neroli to lighten it.

POWDERED INCENSE

Powdered incense can be thrown on a low fire, burned in tiny incense cups of charcoal or in the small braziers available at "head shops" or oriental stores.

Combine one ounce of ground frankincense, one and one-half ounces of ground cascarilla bark, two ounces of powdered benzoin, and one ounce of storax. Grind these together into a coarse powder and moisten with one-half ounce of saltpeter dissolved in one-half ounce of water. Add to this one ounce of alcohol and mix together. Set it aside to dry, then keep in a closed container.

ARABIAN INCENSE POWDER

To five ounces of coarsely ground frankincense, add one-half ounce each of ground cascarilla and benzoin, one-quarter ounce each of ground clove and cassia bark, and one-eighth ounce tincture of musk. Add one-quarter ounce of saltpeter and one ounce of alcohol and mix them well.

Oils of Tolu and vetiver are good in small quantities in most incense. Experiment. Decide what kind of perfume you want: fruity, flowery, woodsy. Large proportions of sandalwood make for an "oriental" scent; oils of neroli and bergamot produce fruity fragrances. If you want perfumes, add rose, jasmine, verbena, honeysuckle. If a spicy outdoor scent is wanted, add oils of carnation, cedar, ginger, sage, nutmeg and the like. The animal essences produce a heavier, more sultry aroma.

ARMENIAN INCENSE PAPERS

Here's another delightful "dry" perfume to try: Cut a large sheet of white blotting paper into about eight pieces. Dissolve one ounce of saltpeter in 12 ounces of boiling water and pull each piece of paper through the solution until it is thoroughly saturated. Hang the strips to dry. Macerate or soak a crushed vanilla bean in eight ounces of alcohol for a week. Filter the solids out. Add to the alcohol 40 drops of oil of lemon grass or 15 of lemon oil, and three ounces tincture of vetiver. Mix this with one and one-half ounces of powdered benzoin and one ounce of crushed sandalwood. Again draw the papers through the resulting liquid and hang them. When dry, cut them into inch-wide strips and store them in waxed paper or foil. To perfume a room, light the paper and immediately blow out the fire. It will smoulder and give off its scent.

The fragrance of these papers can be changed by substituting other oils. Try a few drops of lavender or clove, or of cinnamon or rose.

SWEET RIBBONS

These can be made with inch-wide, woven cotton ribbons, the kind used for upholstery. The ribbon is pulled through the saltpeter mixture, dried and perfumed. It will burn slowly and evenly.

JOSS STICKS

These are difficult to make without a special press. You can obtain one in areas where there is a large oriental population or you can try an old-fashioned potato masher. The idea is to make coils from the paste mixtures. You might roll slim snakes of the paste, place them on waxed paper, and stick tiny twigs into one end so they will stand in an incense holder or glass. You can also try rolling damp paste around a slim twig.

All incense should be kept in a covered container. Although the solids don't lose aroma as quickly as the others, all scented products will "leak" perfume unless kept in closed papers or jars.

Before you begin, you might buy a set of the little charcoal cups and break one into several pieces. These can be ignited and various resins tried out for scent. Be careful of strong oils like clove or cedar and the mints; they can easily take over.

If you don't want to make incense and still like a fragrant room, try your hand at candles.

SCENTED CANDLES

Confucius said, "Incense perfumes bad smells and candles illumine men's hearts."

I have never made candles, relying on my young nephew to supply me with them. When I asked him for information for the book, he supplied the following:

JIMMY'S CANDLES

When making candles, the first step is to get some wax (preferably paraffin), a source of heat, and a can or pot to cook the wax in. An hibachi grill works well but use it outdoors because melting wax smokes and has an unpleasant smell. I usually cook the wax in an old five-pound honey can. This light aluminum seems more heat resistant than, say, a coffee can. Moreover, the can is totally cool less than a minute after it is removed from the heat; that is, the can is cool, the wax is still hot.

Place the can on the heat and put in the wax. It's good to start with thin strips of wax just to get things going. Thin pieces or small chunks melt faster than big chunks. Use an old ax or something of that sort to cut it up. Cook the wax just under boiling (around 225 to 250 degrees). Any hotter will scorch the wax. When you have the desired amount of molten wax, add the coloring and scent. These can be purchased at the same place you buy the wax and wicks (check the classified telephone directory for sources).

Be careful not to put too much of these materials in the wax, particularly color. One or two pinches or less of coloring is enough and two or three drops of scent . . . according to the shade and smell you want and the quantity of wax.

If the wax seems to be getting too hot, take it off the fire. While the wax is simmering, you should grease your mold or dig a hole for sand candles.

❊

SAND CANDLES

Holes should be dug in clean sand because dirt on a sand-cast candle is very unattractive. It is a good idea to wet the sand with water before pouring so it will take shape and won't stick too much. You can also spray the hole with silicone for the same reason . . . experiment!

Dig a hole the shape you want the candle and tie the wick on a stick, letting the loose end dangle into the bottom of the hole. Do not use string. It does not burn correctly. If you want the candle to stand on legs, you can poke three holes in the bottom of the big hole with your fingers or a stick. Be careful to make the holes of equal depth and angle them correctly so as not to have a lopsided candle. After this is done, just pour the wax into the hole over the wick, and wait. It usually takes a candle from one and one-half to two and one-half hours to dry, depending on weather conditions. When a sand-cast candle is dry, dig it up with your hands and brush off as much sand as you can.

❁

MOLDED CANDLES

You can sometimes get these molds where you buy the wax. For a long time people have been greasing molds with corn and similar oils. Motor oil, however, works better. The candle will be shiny, greasy and smooth and will have a built-in gloss.

Prepare the wick for the mold the same as for the sand candle, but put the end through the hole in the bottom of the mold. Wicks seldom fit this hole snugly enough so that no wax escapes. You can eliminate this leakage by shoving a small screw in the hole after the wick is through and pulled taut. If this doesn't work, try using tape.

Now pour the candle, and wait. After the same length of time (one and one-half to two and one-half hours), untie the wick from the stick and tap the mold, open-side-down, on a hard surface. If you used motor oil, the candle should come out almost at once. If you used another oil, it might take quite a beating before the candle comes out. When it's out, wipe the candle off with a cloth and be sure it stands properly. If it doesn't, shave a little off the bottom until it is balanced.

Many hobby shops sell paraffin, wicks scent, and color for making candles. The paraffin runs about $3 for 10 pounds, so you can see the savings possible if you're a candle addict. Beeswax makes the finest, but the cost is proportionately higher.

To perfume the candles, you can use essential oils in small quantity—about one-half ounce to a pound of wax. Do remember to take care with the colors: What looks delicate in a melted wax turns a far darker shade when the candle solidifies.

The scent can be anything you like: I'm partial to cinnamon and jasmine—separately. For a deeper aroma, use two drops to one-half pound of wax of one of the animal tinctures. Try colors that "go with" the scent: pale greens and yellows and roses are lovely. The cinnamon suggests a dark, rich brown.

❀

CHILDREN'S SAND CANDLES

These are good presents or rainy day amusement: Take a flat pan and fill with dampened sand. Let the child press his hand well into the sand leaving a tiny hand-print. Smoothe around it and pour the melted paraffin in over a little wick. Let stand for an hour. For scent, try one of the citrus oils.

ROSE
RECIPES

ROSE BEADS

Gather about 40 roses when they are perfectly dry, chop them fine, and put them in a saucepan just barely covered with water. Use an old iron skillet if you want deep blackish beads. Simmer very gently for about an hour—but never boil. Add water as needed. Let this cool, then re-heat as before. After two good heatings, take the resulting pulp, strain, and form beads with your fingers. Using a large needle with its blunt end stuck in a cork, press each bead down over the needle to make a hole through it. Don't let the bead dry on the needle; it will break as it is removed. When perfectly dry, these beads can be strung and worn. Heat from your neck will cause them to release a pure rose scent. Without the holes, the beads can be tossed in drawers with underclothing.

ROSE BUTTER

Spread the bottom of a covered casserole with a thin layer of fresh butter. Cover with a layer of rose petals. Alternate butter and petals for several layers and cover the dish tightly. Let it remain in a cool place—but not the refrigerator—overnight. The next day, mix the butter and petals and spread on thin rounds of bread topped with a fresh rose. Let the edges of the petals come out beyond the bread. This delicacy is perfect for a tea party for all ages.

CRYSTALLIZED ROSE PETALS

Dissolve two ounces of gum arabic in one-half pint of water. Lay petals of fresh roses on a cookie sheet and sprinkle them with the gum water and a little sugar. Let them dry for 24 hours and put them on plates that will stand a bit of heat. Boil one pound of sugar in one-half pint of water until it reaches 250 degrees (or threads). Keep this sugar well skimmed. Tint it with a bit of coloring—red for roses, pale blue for violets—and pour it over the petals. Leave this for another 24 hours and heat in a barely warm oven until dry. Remove and taste. Then use them to decorate a plain iced cake or cupcake.

ROSE JELLY

Into a kettle with two and one-half quarts of cold water, add two quarts of rose petals; bring to a boil and cook rapidly for 15 minutes. Strain through cloth, reserving the liquid and to it add one-half cup strawberry juice and sufficient water to make two quarts. Add seven pounds of sugar and bring to a rapid boil. Pour in two cups of fruit pectin, all the while stirring. Let this boil for one minute, pack and seal. If the roses haven't imparted enough color, you can add a couple of drops of red food coloring.

POMANDERS

The word pomander comes from the French, *pomme* (apple), and ambergris. Like much of what we have inherited from the past, the perfumed balls we make today are a pale reflection of once-exotic concoctions.

Pliny first described the pomander as being made principally from a combination of cassia, cinnamon, calamus, storax, betel nut, saffron, myrrh, cardamom, balm and wild vine. These ingredients were pounded together and mixed with wine and honey. The mass was put in a perforated case of gold or silver which allowed the scent to escape.

From its purely perfumed use, the pomander came to be thought of as a health aid as cities grew more crowded. Queen Elizabeth was said to have always had one on her person. Here is a recipe from that time from a then-popular play:

"Your only way to make a good pomander is this: Take an ounce of the finest garden mold, cleaned and steeped seven days in change or rose water: then take the best labdanum, benzoin, both storaxes, ambergris, civit and musk: incorporate them together, and work into what form you please. This, if your breath be not too valient, will make you smell as sweet as any lady's dog."*

Pomanders came to be heavily scented with bay leaves which were thought to be helpful in case of plague. Doctors' walking sticks often had compartments which held the various "healthful herbs." Looking back at the recipes necessary to combat odors during those days, one can only tremble at the stenches of the cities. Thomas Wolsey, a sixteenth-century English cardinal, is said to have always carried the shell of an orange filled with spices or a hollowed-out apple full of ground frankincense. It is from these pomanders that ours are derived.

Take a large, fresh orange and punch a lot of holes in it with an ice pick. In each hole put a whole clove until the fruit is completely studded with the spice. Roll the fruit in a mixture of equal parts of powdered orris root and cinnamon to which a few drops of oil of orange have been added. It takes about one and one-half tablespoons of this mixture for each large orange. Wrap the prepared fruit in tissue or foil and set it aside to dry. It will shrink considerably over the weeks. When dry, tie a decorative ribbon or gold cord

*From *The Magic of Herbs* by C. F. Leyel.

around it by which it can hang. You can spruce up its appearance with a bit of holly leaf for Christmas or an artificial flower and leaf or two. Give the pomanders as presents to hang in a closet or pantry.

There are perforated china balls made for pomanders that are also very nice filled with sachet or potpourri. They are hung wherever you want their fragrance released.

And to ward off insomnia, here's a fanciful solution: "An apple to make one sleep is made of all these: opium, mandrake, juyce of hemlock, henbane seed, wine lees, to which must be added musk that by the scent it may prooke him who smels unto it. Make a ball as big as a man may grasp in his hand: by often smelling to this it will cause him to shut his eyes and fall asleep."*

*From *The Magic of Herbs* by C. F. Leyel.

PART III

INTO THE

KITCHEN

My permanent sense-memory of the Christmas season comes from my mother's yearly baking of fruitcakes from a recipe now well over 100 years old. For each 15 pounds of cake, she added a teaspoon each of cinnamon, allspice, ground cloves and nutmeg. Into the batter, rich, yellow, thick, and impossible to mix except with the bare hands, also went orange and lemon peel and three pounds of muscat raisins which had been soaked overnight in wine. The baking of these cakes perfumed the house for days, leading us children in mounting excitement towards Christmas.

However, we need not wait for the holiday kitchen to make the house fragrant; most of us have that opportunity every day as many of the ingredients used to impart scent to potpourris and sachets will also add immeasurably to both the flavor and aroma of what we cook. The scent of herbs and spices wafting from the kitchen create appetites for even the most ordinary dishes.

There is such a multitude of herbs and spices and citrus to add to recipes that I will limit my suggestions to only those mentioned in the text for perfumery; so when you buy or grow, save or find these for your potpourris, you will be able to try them in the kitchen as well.

CITRUS AND MINTS

Let me start with my own favorites, citrus and the mints. What can you do with them? What *can't* you! The obvious, fresh mint in tea, hot or cold. The not-so-obvious, fresh mint chopped into green peas as they come off the burner, stirred gently, served with butter. To make a nice sauce for lamb or duck, gently mash a jar of red currant jelly in a bowl, scissor in five teaspoons of fresh mint, one tablespoon each of grated orange and lemon rind. You can add half as much of the same cut and grated ingredients to a jar of softened grape jelly for another good garnish. Give prepared mint jelly a lift by adding these fresh ingredients. And a little chopping of fresh mint can be added to mushrooms you are cooking for meat sauces.

Citrus Candy

Now, for the best candy in the world: It also has the advantage of the bioflavinoids remaining in the peel so you will feel less uneasy about children gorging on it. Make this with any of the citrus rinds; the big, thick-skinned California grapefruits are fine as are oranges, big lemons and limes. Tangerines take less cooking and have a more mellow flavor. The ingredients given are for the equivalent of four big oranges.

Make lengthwise cuts in the peels and remove them from the fruit; put the peelings of cold water to cover, then bring to a boil. Reduce the heat and simmer until it becomes soft. Drain away the water, scrape the white membrane from the peels, and with a knife or scissors, cut them into narrow strips. These strips go back into the saucepan with one cup of sugar, one-half cup water, and two tablespoons of corn syrup, which is all cooked slowly until it comes clear or registers 240 degrees on the candy thermometer. Take the peels out one at a time and arrange them to cool on several plates. When they are just cool, roll them in granulated sugar and store on layers of waxed paper. As the peels keep their color, they also make a lovely looking gift box.

Here's **marjoram** and **lemon** in a fast-made jelly: Pour one cup of boiling water over two tablespoons of fresh marjoram and let it stand, covered, for one-half hour. Strain this water into a large enamel saucepan. Add three cups of sugar and one-third cup of fresh lemon juice; stir until dissolved. Bring quickly to a boil and pour in one-half cup of bottled pectin, stirring constantly. Bring to a boil again and allow to boil for one-half minute. Take from the heat, skim well, pack and seal the jelly.

Citrus rind, grated, can be added to most cakes and other sweets to great advantage. I often grate orange peel into fudge instead of using nuts; it's different and good. The next time tangerine season comes around, save and dry some of the peels. It is the most subtle of the citrus, blends delightfully with gravies and sauces for meats and poultry, and smells delicious while cooking. My motto: When in doubt, grate citrus.

You will likely be buying sticks of **cinnamon** and **vanilla** for various scented products; see what a difference these fresh spices can make in your cooking. A vanilla bean has many uses; a small piece broken off and added to the hot liquid (for custards and puddings) imparts a light, lovely taste. A bean, split and ground with an equal amount of sugar, then added to two cups of additional sugar and all tightly sealed, will take the place of more vanilla in many recipes. You can also do this with sugar and grated orange or lemon rind for extra-good baked goodies.

Cinnamon sticks go into many hot drinks, combining equally well with apple, rum, teas, coffees, chocolate, and hot toddies of many persuasions; the Chinese use it in preparing "red-cooked" meats.

Powdered **coriander** is an essential for good Indian curry and adds something special to a cake mix. Before we go into the herb family, let me mention that some of the essential oils you buy for scent purposes can also be used for cooking—very sparingly. Remember that the more the herb, root, seed, flower, or what-have-you is concentrated, the stronger it will become. Thus, a fresh leaf should be used in greater quantity than the same, dried; when developed into an essential oil, the flavor-scent component is geometrically multiplied.

OILS (to cook with)

almond	lime
cinnamon	orange, bitter
clove	orange, sweet
grapefruit	peppermint
lemon	rosemary
tangerine	

HERBS (to cook with)

Rosemary adds to all meats: beef, pork, lamb and veal. A bit crushed and sprinkled over a roast after it is cooked makes it fragrant on the way to the table. Rosemary can also be added to the pan gravy just before serving. As the essential oils are quickly given up in heat, don't boil their goodness away with prolonged cooking. Rosemary is also nice in jellies and, surprisingly, finely ground, as an addition to biscuits.

Thyme goes well with beef and veal, is essential for a tasty poultry dressing, can be snipped up in salads, flavors onions and fish, is used as a seasoning for vegetable juices and soup—and is always in clam chowder. Use **marjoram**, alone, or mixed with thyme, in spinach, tomatoes, string beans, and always with lamb.

I've already waxed lyrical about **basil** as a superior scent herb; I also use it frequently in the kitchen. Basil goes with anything containing tomatoes, cooked or raw; it belongs with cheese, is necessary for a good spaghetti sauce; it's fine in green beans, carrots, peas, potatoes, and with beef and pork dishes, particularly stews.

Dill goes with lamb and in sauces for other meat and poultry; it's also good with fish and in salad dressings. A few seeds will perk up an apple pie, and it's a nice addition to cream and cottage cheeses.

Fennel is good in salads, in beets and cabbage; its little seeds can be sparingly added to puddings and cakes.

Caraway seeds we know from rye bread, of course; now try them in cole slaw, in cooked cabbage and biscuits. When you can get the fresh foliage, it makes a lovely garnish for a roast.

Any of the herbs that have an affinity for beef can be used to perk up and glamorize hamburgers and meatloaf. You will be surprised at the difference their addition makes. Don't neglect the herb jars when you are using canned vegetables and soups. For vegetables, drain half the water from the can, add your herb, heat gently and serve with butter. When basil is added to canned beans, the only way to tell they aren't fresh is that canned beans never seem to have strings.

TEAS

Many herbs produce good teas; you need fresh or dried herbs, a china or enamel kettle and boiling water. On a tablespoon of dry herbs or a handful of fresh herbs, pour two cups of boiling water and allow to stand for a few minutes. All the mints make lovely tea as do lemon verbena, anise seed, rosemary, marjoram, and, for novelty of taste and aroma, add a little grated citrus, a few rose petals, or even a pinch of lavender. Let your sense of smell dictate; whatever appeals to your nose will doubtless make a pleasant drink.

ADDENDUM

HERB SMOKING MIXTURE:
TAIZ OF TUCSON

If you're trying to stop smoking tobacco and can't break all the physical habits—lighting up, holding a cigarette in your mouth—try this substitute. You'll have to roll your own, but that isn't a bad idea either, as it takes time and trouble.

To one ounce of red clover tops add one ounce of coltsfoot, and one-quarter ounce each of thyme, rosemary, yerba santa and lavender flowers. Tear everything until it's about the right size for "tobacco" and store in a closed container.

PART IV

SCENTED PRODUCTS FOR
FUND RAISING

There is no better way to raise money for your charitable organization than by making and selling fragrant potpourris, sachets, pomanders, place cards with pressed flowers, and bath potpourris. All of these items make acceptable gifts, "thank you's" for a hostess; and a big potpourri is a grand present.

Begin collecting in early spring. Save every bit of floral material you can grow or find. Experiment with everything; most won't have a fragrance but can be used, pressed or dried, as decoration for potpourris and place cards. From the garden, gather marigolds and bachelor buttons; press pansies and daisies; carnations, and some asters, retain color when pulled loose and dried. Press flowerets from Queen Anne's lace, thistle flower, little sheaves of grasses with their flowers. Save some peelings from citrus; pick and dry all of your mints and other herbs. Plant some lemongrass early in spring for fall harvest. And, of course, every rose you can grow or beg.

Order ground orris root, lavender, and some essential oils from a supplier, and find a box manufacturer who will sell in small quantities the type and size of boxes you will want. Collect scraps of ribbon; check with a variety store for potpourri containers by the case. Perhaps some of the old-fashioned stickers being sold will add to your boxes or glass containers. If you go to the beach, look for seashells large enough to hold potpourri or sachet under a plastic-wrap cover. During the height of citrus season, start making pomanders for Christmas. Begin making sachet cases of scraps: gingham, silks and the silk-like synthetics, whatever appeals to you. Someone good with the needle can start embroidering, putting lacy edges on the little pillows to have them ready for their sachet filling.

Your organization's decision on which products to make will be based on the quantity of flower materials available to the members, and how much investment you want to make initially in containers, materials from the herb houses and boxes. The most expensive to make is also the most profitable. A good potpourri in an attractive jar will sell anywhere from five to twelve dollars, depending on the container and what your market will bear. And when you make potpourri, the bottom of the barrel, so to speak, is an excellent sachet, so that you can have, with one large batch, both the expensive and more reasonable items to sell. Box manufacturers usually have white boxes for candies that cost only a few cents each when bought in any quantity for sachets. Or you can use plastic bags tied with ribbons for even less expense. Small baskets for bunches of gingham-covered sachets run under one dollar. These little baskets can also be used for small potpourris covered by net and tied with ribbons. Bath potpourris can be packaged in net bags with big fluffs at the top.

Your pomanders should go into small white boxes in tissue paper where they nestle colorfully. If they are for Christmas, decorate with a holly sprig; for other times, use a bright orange ribbon or a dark green velvet tie.

Small decorated tin boxes are available for homemade teas. Label each one with the ingredients.

As a general, ball-park figure, a two-dollar investment in materials, containers, and such should return about five dollars for your fund raising. The more you can grow and develop yourself, of course, the less the cost. If you create your own oils, grind your own orris root, and dry your own herbs, the only cost will be for whatever containers you choose to package your products in.

 # SOURCES

Three sources for materials needed to make most of the products in this book are:

On the west coast: *Natures' Herbs*
281 Ellis Street
San Francisco, California

On the east coast: *Aphrodisia*
28 Carmine Street
New York, New York

Caswell-Massey Co., Ltd.
320 West 13th Street (catalogue)
575 Lexington Avenue (to visit)
New York, New York

Of the three, Natures' Herbs and Aphrodisia are comparable in prices; Caswell-Massey is far more costly, but they have some extra-fine materials. However, they all carry good products.